Crime in Fact and Fiction

Brian P Block

 **WATERSIDE** PRESS

Crime in Fact and Fiction
by Brian P Block

ISBN 978-1-909976-22-1 (Paperback)
ISBN 978-1-906534-35-6 (Epub ebook)
ISBN 978-1-906534-36-3 (Adobe ebook)

Main UK distributor Gardners Books, 1 Whittle Drive, Eastbourne, East Sussex, BN23 6QH. Tel: +44 (0)1323 521777; sales@gardners.com; www.gardners.com

North American distribution Ingram Book Company, One Ingram Blvd, La Vergne, TN 37086, USA. Tel: (+1) 615 793 5000; inquiry@ingramcontent.com

Cataloguing-In-Publication Data A catalogue record for this book can be obtained from the British Library.

Printed by Lightning Source.

e-book *Crime in Fact and Fiction* is available as an ebook and also to subscribers of Myilibrary, Dawsonera, ebrary, and Ebscohost.

Published 2015 by
Waterside Press
Sherfield Gables
Sherfield-on-Loddon
Hook, Hampshire
United Kingdom RG27 0JG

Telephone +44(0)1256 882250
E-mail enquiries@watersidepress.co.uk
Online catalogue WatersidePress.co.uk

Table of Contents

About the author

Brian P Block holds degrees in pharmacy, pharmacology, Chinese, criminology, law and history of science from London, Brunel and Westminster Universities and the Inns of Court School of Law. Two things confer on the author his unique perspective in writing this book: he was a justice of the peace for many years; and he spent his professional career testing the safety of new medicines. A Fullbright and post-doctoral scholar at Yale University, USA he has been a frequent contributor to legal journals. He is the author of three previous Waterside Press publications: *Hanging in the Balance: A History of the Abolition of Capital Punishment in Britain* (1997), *Famous Cases: Nine Trials that Changed the Law* (2000) (both written together with John Hostettler) and *The Pain and the Pride: Life Inside the Colorado Boot Camp* (2002).

To the memory of the late J D ('Zitch') Shivas, an outstandingly talented teacher of English at Raine's Foundation Grammar School, who did not so much teach English but acquainted us with its delights.

Introduction

Many novels, plays and films on TV or in the cinema are detective stories or thrillers and some are 'courtroom dramas'. Mostly, but not always, the criminals get their comeuppance and good triumphs over evil. On the page, screen or stage many of the plots are largely to do with crime, detection and bringing the criminal to justice; but often the storylines have nothing to do with criminals, police or lawyers but are more about *injustice*. These are more subtle and demonstrate that it is not necessary to have crime in order to have justice, and often show that social injustice often leads to crime and is just as often the result of crime. But what is even more interesting is that the depiction of the police and detection bears little resemblance to how police detectives operate in real life; that court procedure in fiction is not a fair depiction of what actually goes on in a courtroom but is often outrageously wide of the mark; and that where on television methodology involving fingerprints, handwriting, material evidence (such as fibres, drug or poison traces), injuries, blood splatter patterns and complex forensic science applied to substances or dead bodies is shown, it is frequently so simplistic as to be risible. However, this is not the case with the written word when recorded by pathologists.

It is this disjunction between what really goes on and what is shown or written about that is fascinating. I have been told by people working in television that the programmes are not written with people like me in mind but to entertain the general public who are not interested in verisimilitude and are not at all surprised that a young girl in her twenties is capable of performing the entire gamut of forensic examination from handwriting to DNA-analysis that it would take a team of highly qualified forensic scientists to do. They do not care that one clever detective could solve a crime that would require an entire local police force. They do not notice or are indifferent when characters talk about milligrams when they mean micrograms.

This book is not intended to be an academic tome; there are already many books that are. It is meant to show, with examples, that what actually goes on in the criminal justice system is rarely accurately depicted in fiction. That is not to imply that the fiction which contains these inaccuracies is necessarily bad: some of the greatest novels and plays ever written fictionalise what actually goes on in the real world and get it wrong. This is a tricky tightrope for writers. They are, after all, writing fiction and fiction does not have to be four square with fact. But there is always a danger that the fiction can depart so far from fact that it makes the reader or viewer uneasy, or worse, stop reading, switch off or walk out of the theatre at the interval.

One reason why this does not happen as often as it might is that the reader, viewer or theatre-goer has little experience of how the real system actually operates and therefore does not realise that what is being read or viewed is inaccurate, wrong or even derisory. Examples of the differences between what actually happens (fact) and what is shown or written (fiction) will be used to demonstrate the difference between what is real and what is made up.

It is probably fair to say that many people reading a book or watching a play realise but do not really care that what is being shown is not a reflection of what actually happens. After all, they are watching or reading fiction not a play or book explaining the law or how a criminal trial is conducted. There is nothing wrong with this attitude and all fiction requires a certain degree of suspension of disbelief. Who, reading *Wind in the Willows,* dismisses it because animals cannot talk? Who would switch off a TV programme about battles in World War Two because German soldiers do not really speak in broken English? Who would consider *Twelfth Night* nonsense because no characters in the play would really be deceived by (the female) Viola pretending to be (the male) Cesario? But if Ratty and Mole were depicted as astro-physicists, if the German soldiers delivered all their lines in fluent English, or if Olivia, who is in love with 'Cesario', failed to notice during an amorous embrace that there was *tout le monde au balcon* but nothing in the cellar it is fair to speculate that there would be a very high order of disbelief.

Although people who watch or read fiction realise that what they are watching or reading is not quite the same thing as what actually happens, they generally do not mind if it helps the plot along. Where there might, or should, be serious objections is when the plot *depends* on a marked departure from what would happen in real life and this happens from time to time in detective programmes shown on TV.

One further problem with fictionalised presentations of criminal justice, particularly those that take place largely in the courtroom, is the terminology. As will be shown, words such as 'justice', 'truth', 'guilt', 'innocent' and 'reasonable doubt' are used frequently as if they had a definitive meaning. They do each have a meaning but they do not all mean the same thing to different people. There is often a consensus so that life in the courts can go on but, as we shall see, many of these words, which are important in trials, are abstract and thus difficult to pin down. This can sometimes be resolved by references to precedent.

Barrister: 'The court may not be clear regarding the degree of criminality of the defendant but it may be illuminating if your Lordship would draw the attention of the jury to the similar case of *R v Criminal Bastard 1898* in which Lord Justice Legalmind ruled…'. Precedent can cut through philosophical arguments like a whetted knife as it avoids attempting to resolve the meanings of words that have no real meaning by resorting to what someone else said a century or a year ago.

It is accepted that trades and professions all have their own jargon. Scientists have jargon that non-scientists cannot understand. Moreover, scientists from different branches of science cannot understand each others' jargon: biologists do not usually understand the words that are used in subatomic physics; oceanographers are unlikely to understand the lexicon of palaeontologists. But generally speaking most people working in the same discipline understand each other. Sociologists, whose vocabulary is like a foreign language to non-sociologists are readily understood by other sociologists. This is true of lawyers. Lawyers understand such terms as 'arrest', 'caution' and 'criminal offence'; so do most people who are not lawyers. Other jargon words such as 'indictment', 'mitigation' and 'no case to answer' are all understood by lawyers but not by most non-lawyers. To take this to an extreme there are legal words and phrases in Latin such as *mens rea*, *res gestae* and *locus delicti* that many younger lawyers may not understand as they are used less and less. But there are also words and phrases in ordinary English that everyone, lawyers and non-lawyers alike, understand, but are sometimes understood differently by different people; or more often not understood because the words and phrases in question are not definitive like 'prison' or 'young offender institution' or 'sexual assault' but are conceptual like 'truth', 'innocent' and 'not guilty'. These philosophical constructs which seem so easy to understand are a minefield through which I struggled to find a path during my many years as a magistrate.

∾

When I was invited to apply to be a magistrate I gave it some serious thought for approximately five milliseconds before agreeing. I had little idea of what was entailed; I had been inside a court only once when a friend was accused of driving faster than the speed limit permitted. I noticed that the police prosecuted and that there were three people sitting at an elevated bench who decided if my friend was guilty or not, and if he was, what punishment to give him. He pleaded guilty and was fined five pounds. Those were the days!

Thinking it over in the few days before I made my formal application I thought that being a magistrate—a justice of the peace, no less, which sounded better even though it means the same thing—was right up my street or, to put it in the jargon I was soon to acquire, appropriate to my background and qualifications. I was not a lawyer and had not been particularly interested in the law, or justice or the courts. I am a scientist and what a scientist does all the time is to gather evidence either by experiment or observation or both, arrive at a conclusion, or hypothesis, or theorem and then test the conclusion by more experiments or data-gathering. One also publishes what has been discovered and the means used, in order that other scientists can test your method and results. So, I thought to myself, 'What do magistrates do? Sort through the evidence presented to them and arrive at a conclusion as to whether the defendant is guilty or not. You do not even have to publish your results and invite other magistrates to find fault with your reasoning. I can do that; pity I'd have to do it with two other people. I'd prefer to do it by myself.'

So I applied and was interviewed. The interview seemed to go well and I was next invited to appear before the Advisory Committee on the Appointment of Magistrates. There were about a dozen or fifteen of them sitting at a long table, with me at the other side. They asked me some practical questions about my background, my work, whether I could get time off to sit in court, whether I was married and so on. I could answer those. Then I was asked hypothetical questions: would I have difficulty sending someone to prison? No, I thought. Just say, 'You will go to prison for three months'. But thinking they would prefer something a little more fancy, I replied to the effect that if their crime was serious enough to merit a term of imprisonment I would not shirk from sentencing the defendant to it. That seemed to go down well, judging by the nodding and muttering of the committee; but their reaction appeared to indicate that they believed that prison was merely a poor substitute for the gallows. A few other questions followed, about drink driving, drug taking and other forms of misbehaviour. Then it was all over. They thanked me for coming and indicated that I was to leave.

I left, not knowing whether I had passed, whether I was a magistrate or not and having no idea what would happen next. Nothing happened, not for weeks and then months. I assumed that I had not passed and that my magisterial career had ended before it got going.

Then suddenly, without warning, without hint, months later I received a letter from the Lord Chancellor, no less. It said, 'I am minded to appoint you as one of Her Majesty's Justices' and if I was still interested I should fill in the accompanying form and send it back. I was intrigued by the quaint wording; I had expected that if I had passed I would have received a note saying that I was hereby appointed ... etc. But re-reading the letter I had an image of the Lord Chancellor coming down to breakfast and saying to his wife who was busy with the toaster,

'You know, my dear, I've been thinking and I'm minded to appoint this Block chappie as a JP. What do you think?'

'What can I think?' she would reply. 'You are the Lord Chancellor and I only make the toast. Yeah, give him a go. Can't be any worse than some of the ... ' But I digress.

I filled in and returned the form and learned that I was appointed to an outer-London court in the Middlesex area of greater London. Sometime later I was instructed to present myself at the Middlesex Guildhall in order to take the oath of allegiance and judicial oath. One had a choice either to 'swear by Almighty God' or to 'solemnly, sincerely and truly affirm and declare' to be 'faithful and bear true allegiance to the Queen' and her successors. This was the oath of allegiance. Then came the judicial oath; one swore or declared 'to truly serve' the Queen 'in the office of justice of the peace' and to 'do right to all manner of people after the laws and usages of the realm without fear or favour, affection or ill-will'. I read the oaths, and I was in, a JP according to the Justices of the Peace Act 1361.

I liked the bit in the judicial oath about fear or favour, affection or ill-will but the split infinitive that preceded it stuck in the gullet. However, I just about had enough sense not to alter it as I read it out loud, and in retrospect it is clear that one could dispense with 'truly' altogether: you either served HMQ or you did not unless you did so half-heartedly, in which case 'to serve the Queen wholeheartedly' would not only read better but actually mean something.

Participating in the criminal justice system gave me a great deal of satisfaction as I believed I knew what 'justice' was. It was when somebody who had done something against the law, committed a crime, was caught by the police, taken to court, tried according to the law and found guilty, in which case a punishment was imposed; or found to be not guilty, in which case he or she was not punished and was free to go. Justice, for me was a philosophical abstract construct made flesh in a court of law. There were normally only two outcomes in a court case, guilty or its antonym, not guilty. It was to be some time before I realised that the real antonym to guilty is innocent, but that is not an option at the end of an English trial.

It is rather odd, though it did not occur to me at the time, that neither the word nor the reality of 'being innocent' plays any part in the criminal trial. Odd, because one of the early concepts of which we were made aware, and which was frequently emphasised, was vested in the hallowed phrase 'presumption of innocence'. This was taken to mean that before the trial began, and indeed during the trial, the accused is presumed to be innocent of the offence or offences with which he or she was charged. No matter how trivial or serious they were, how much he or she looked or behaved like a rogue, or how many convictions they might have already (but the magistrates, unless there are specific circumstances, are not told of previous convictions unless and until they return a guilty plea), we were to presume that the man or woman standing before us was innocent. And yet, at the end of the trial, no matter how trivial was the evidence against him or her, irrespective of how upstanding a citizen the defendant was shown to be, despite the fact that there had been no previous convictions (we were allowed to be told if that was the case). I never once heard a bench chairman then announce, 'We find that you are completely innocent and you are free to go'. Instead, invariably, 'We find that you are not guilty...' Not innocent, yet not guilty; and within this small lacuna between the two phrases sits 'reasonable doubt', an abstraction linking two other abstractions.

On the wall behind many a court bench, in full view of the public, is a coat of arms bearing the motto *Honi soit qui mal y pense* (He who thinks evil is evil) which is almost a presumption of guilt. A better depiction of the law's fascination with abstractions would be Prospero's comment at the end of Shakespeare's *The Tempest*: 'We are such stuff as dreams are made on ...'

Just when I thought I had understood the concept of guilty and not guilty and was rejoicing in the realisation that a verdict could be only one or the other, a new modification was introduced. When during a training exercise we were asked how the concept of guilty could, or should, be qualified at the end of a trial somebody suggested 'guilty or bloody guilty' which was not the desired answer. The preferred answer was, and still is, guilty beyond reasonable doubt. Of course, we all said, nobody can be certain if the defendant is guilty unless he or she pleads guilty, but if we doubt his or her guilt having heard all the evidence, we must deliver a not guilty verdict. But the doubt must be reasonable, our instructor emphasised; of course, we said, we cannot let the defendant off if our doubt is unreasonable. There was some enthusiasm at this point for there being a presumption of *guilt* which if appropriate could be gradually eroded by doubt and when the doubt became reasonable we would let him off. In retrospect it is clear that we did not know what we were talking about and the legal adviser who was instructing us must have been glad to get away before we found him guilty of something.

During the weeks and months that followed my understanding of the concept of justice was crumbling; it was clear that an action or a decision could not only be just or unjust. In court, one must find a defendant guilty *beyond reasonable doubt* or say that he is not guilty, but we do not have to conclude that a defendant is *not guilty* beyond reasonable doubt. Having jumped that hurdle I was confronted with the question, what is 'reasonable'? If a defence lawyer shows that from where the police officer who gave evidence was standing, and given that it was getting dark, he could not clearly discern the colour of the sweater that the man who threw the brick through the window was wearing, is that reasonable doubt? Or does one think, who cares about the colour of the sweater, the policeman says it is the defendant? After all, policemen do not tell lies. In which case, no doubt. Or if you consider that the policeman's evidence is flawed because three witnesses have independently told the court that the defendant was attending his own wedding at the time of the break-in, there must be doubt amounting to total disbelief that the defendant is guilty.

This insoluble conundrum has been I think best presented by Henry Cecil who was himself a judge and also a prolific author. In his book *According to the Evidence*, published in 1954 there is an episode where at the end of a trial for murder the jury is sent out to reach a verdict and the following conversation ensues.

'Before we retire,' said the foreman, who was a professor of metaphysics, 'may I ask your Lordship for some enlightenment?'

'What is your question?' asked the judge.

'Your Lordship said that before the jury can convict we must feel sure of the prisoner's guilt. May I ask your Lordship exactly what "feel sure" means?'

'It means what it says', said the judge, rather testily. Before you can convict, you must feel quite sure.'

I'm sorry to trouble your Lordship', went on the foreman, 'but I would be grateful for some help. The jury feel quite sure they are trying this case. Have they to be as sure of the prisoner's guilt as that?'

'No, of course not', said the judge.

'Well, my Lord, when I asked your Lordship what "sure" meant, you said "quite sure", but now you seem to be saying that it means "not quite sure". It's a little confusing for the jury. I always used to read that the prosecution had to prove its case beyond reasonable doubt.'

'So it has', said the judge, and he added, recognising a look on the foreman's face, 'you may not ask me what that means.' The judge finally got himself out of this maze by saying that 'Before convicting a man, a jury must feel as sure of his guilt as they can feel sure of anything which they have not plainly seen for themselves'—which is as good an explanation as I have heard.

Having grasped that nettle and decided the sort of thing *for me* that would constitute reasonable doubt I briefly wondered why the cumbersome 'not guilty' was used: why not just 'innocent'? What is the difference between 'not guilty' and 'innocent'? 'Not guilty' is a finding by magistrates or a jury; innocence is a fact in the real world. But just because it is a real fact it does not follow that anybody recognises it. A shoplifter is brought to court and evidence against him or her is presented. His or her defence is that he or she stole nothing and the 'stolen' goods were slipped into their bag by another person. The bench find the defence plausible and although they recognise that the accused person could be lying, they have a reasonable doubt that he or she stole the goods and *declare* that he or she is not guilty. The lying defendant, however, *knows* that he or she took the items without paying; thus he or she is 'not guilty' but nor is he or she innocent. 'Not guilty' is a human construct but 'innocence' is an existential fact, even if nobody is aware of it. Our defendant is not guilty in court but guilty in the real world, and he or she is the only one who knows it. This complexity is further concatenated when public opinion indicates that the public believe (or 'know') a defendant is guilty but the police just couldn't prove it.

So we are left with 'guilty', 'not guilty', 'innocent' and 'guilty but they couldn't prove it'. There are also subtle distinctions such as 'guilty but they [the jury, magistrates] are too soft so they let him off'. Added to this list of abstractions is 'reasonable'. What is the distinction between 'doubt' and '*reasonable* doubt'? Lord Denning answered this question by saying that 'reasonable doubt' did not mean 'a scintilla of doubt': thus replacing one abstraction with another. The word 'scintilla' comes from the Latin for 'spark' and has been defined as 'a tiny amount of something', a 'trace', a 'minute amount'. What he was really saying was that one could find a defendant guilty even if the doubt was more than a scintilla, but presumably less than reasonable. What a wonderful lexicon that would be, to announce at the end of a trial: 'We doubt whether you are guilty but although our doubt is more than a scintilla it is less than reasonable so we find you guilty as accused'. The poor, baffled defendant would be glad to get into the comfort of a cell.

From all this we can deduce that 'reasonable doubt' is more than a 'scintilla of doubt' and that in practical terms—for although justice is abstract verdicts are real—jurors and magistrates may have a tiny amount of doubt about the defendant's guilt but still find him or her guilty as charged.

Although all participants in a trial swear or affirm that they will tell the truth, at the end nobody knows what the truth really is, except for the defendant. It is said that the accusatorial system gets to the truth by the two sides hammering out the evidence. But if the prosecutor proves his case beyond reasonable doubt, has the truth come out? Or has he been better at persuading the jury or magistrates that his or her evidence is closer to the truth than that of the defence? It is clear, then, that being *concerned* with getting to the truth is not the same as *actually* getting to the truth. The truth is only reached when the verdict coincides with the actuality: for example, when an innocent defendant is found not guilty. If a defendant who really committed the offence is found not guilty he or she can shout out with impunity (but cannot ordinarily be tried twice for the same offence) 'You are all wrong! I did it!' Thus it is clear that the tribunal never decides if a defendant is guilty or innocent; all that can be decided is whether the prosecution has proved its case or not beyond reasonable doubt.

It is extremely rare, if it happens at all, that a jury can have serious (more than reasonable) doubt about a defendant's guilt yet still return a verdict of guilty; such an event would provoke an immediate appeal by the defence and if doubt could be shown the verdict would be overturned. This is even less likely to occur in the magistrates' court because the court legal adviser (sometimes, especially in the past called the court clerk), who is present to ensure among other things that trials are properly run and to advise the justices on the law, would be very quick to notice that there were serious doubts that perhaps the justices had not noticed or chose to ignore, and would point these out in the privacy of the justices' retiring room. Advice from the clerk to acquit would be rarely ignored but if the magistrates defied the clerk and convicted the defendant the clerk would advise the defence lawyer, should it be needed, who might then lodge an appeal to the Crown Court or the

High Court of Justice if it was a legal matter.

However, the reverse can and occasionally does, take place: the jury realises that the defendant is guilty according to the law but for reasons of its own disapproves strongly of the law under which this is the case, or believes the defendant acted reasonably even if his or her action was unlawful, or think that they would do the same in similar circumstances—and they nevertheless acquit. This situation is commonly called a 'perverse verdict' and when 'not guilty' is unexpectedly announced none of the lawyers in court are able to do anything about it. Such cases are not as uncommon as might be imagined and often involve the defendant having attacked the victim who was engaged in criminal activity such as burglary with far more force than needed to make the burglar desist, resulting in serious injury or death. The defendant is charged with manslaughter or causing grievous bodily harm but the jury thinks 'serve the victim right' and lets the defendant off. Other cases have involved demonstrators charged with public order offences during a protest the aims of which the jury approves; the demonstrators have clearly broken the law but are acquitted.

An interesting instance of a perverse verdict occurred a few years ago not in a court of law but on television. In the programme 'Strictly Come Dancing' a number of couples dance and after each has done so a panel of four expert judges each award a mark out of ten, so the total mark is out of 40. To make the competition more interesting—or possibly to make it interesting at all—each couple consists of one expert dancer and one amateur who has never danced at this level before and who is coached by his or her professional partner. Each week the couple with the lowest total mark is eliminated from the competition. However, the judges' marks account for only half the total; in the following 24 hours members of the public can phone in their votes and that makes up the other half of the vote. In one series one of the dancers was the sometime BBC foreign correspondent John Sergeant who danced with a professional dancer called Kristina. Mr Sergeant was a lousy dancer but had a lovely personality. He danced his dance with the forbearing Kristina and they then went up to the judges' table where they were excoriated and their total marks struggled to rise to double figures. Some of the judges directed their abuse at Sergeant: there was nothing wrong with Kristina's dancing as she was an expert. Throughout this extreme belittlement and denigration

Mr Sergeant stood there with a beatific smile and said not a word. The public loved it; and furthermore they loved John Sergeant. Each week he and Kristina received from the public bucketfuls of votes that kept them in the competition. This was a perverse verdict on a grand scale. The problem was that in order for Sergeant and his partner to remain in the competition two better dancers who had higher scores from the judges had to be eliminated. The problem was solved when after a number of weeks of public support to keep him in the competition and—a great and genuine fear of wrecking the show for ballroom dancing enthusiasts, possibly even Seargeat and Kristina winning—they voluntarily withdrew from the competition to the disappointment of the public and no doubt the relief of the programme makers. The public cared little for dancing skills: they loved John Sergeant. They voted not for ability but entertainment. They did not vote for what they were asked to vote for: their verdict was perverse.

I think this situation is extremely rare in the magistrates' court. There are several reasons for this. Magistrates usually sit in threes and a two to one verdict is legally acceptable and correct. If all three justices are agreed on acquittal in spite of the evidence against the defendant they will return to the court intending to deliver a not guilty verdict. The legal adviser will likely meet them before they enter the courtroom and ask what they have decided. Realising what has happened he or she will point out that they are ignoring sound evidence and flying in the face of the law, on which he or she is qualified and there to advise. If there is a two to one decision to acquit, the 'odd man out' may ask the adviser to come into the retiring room and point out his or her misgivings, and again the latter will advise the magistrates about the law, and reiterate the evidence against the defendant. He or she might even remind them of their judicial oath: to do right... without fear or favour.

How can juries get away with this whereas magistrates nearly always do not? There are several explanations. After the judge's summing-up of the case the jury is left alone unless they ask the judge about a point of law or for some other legitimate clarification. Once the jury informs the court that it has reached a verdict, nobody asks—not the judge nor the defence or prosecution lawyers—what that verdict is. When it has reached a verdict the jurors return to the courtroom and all but their foreman sit; the foreman remains standing and the clerk to the Crown Court asks, 'What is your verdict?' and the foreman replies either 'Guilty' or 'Not guilty'. Once a not guilty verdict is announced it stands; it cannot be reversed.

Furthermore, jurors are probably braver than magistrates. They deliver their verdict and go home; in many instances they are unlikely to serve on a jury again especially if excused by the judge. Magistrates, on the other hand, are there for the long haul, week after week, year after year. And before they give their (perverse) verdict in court the legal adviser will ask what they have decided, quickly detect their motive and attempt to deter them. They can still defy his or her advice but when it is backed by some reference to the law and to the evidence they would be both brave and foolish to ignore it and indeed could be held liable in damages.

However, sometimes magistrates can still find a way to swim against the tide and two instances illustrate this. One case involved an outpatient at the A & E of the local hospital slapping a nurse in the face because he was not being seen quickly enough. He pleaded guilty, apologised and his solicitor struggled to find an excuse (known as mitigation). The normal sentence for an offence of this kind was a substantial fine or to ask for a probation report. But we wanted to send a message to the hospital staff and to the local population that this behaviour would not be tolerated and to the astonishment of the defendant and his lawyer we sent him to prison for three months. Although strictly this sentence flew in the face of the guidelines the adviser later indicated his approval to the magistrates involved.

In another case a young man was accused of parking a motor vehicle on a road without it being insured. He was persuaded by the adviser to plead guilty as he had no defence: it was a car, it was on a public road, it was not insured. The defendant explained that his hobby was to find very old cars in poor condition and repair them. He had towed the car in question and parked it outside his house intending to tow it to a garage he rented. Unfortunately, the police had noticed it first, before he towed it away. We accepted his explanation and decided not to impose a penalty and explained that we had no authority not to award penalty points and gave him the minimum of six. As he left the court my colleague said to me that the man was a bus driver. I called to the usher to get him back into court, and back he came looking tearful. The adviser established that he was indeed a bus driver and asked him what might happen as he now had points on his licence. He replied that it meant automatic dismissal; drivers had to have a perfectly clean licence. At this point the prosecutor stood up and asked for the case to be reopened. I replied that it was probably not necessary as we could find 'special reasons' for not awarding points even though strictly there probably were none in this case. The prosecutor persisted and despite the normal functus officio rule already mentioned decided that I could in this instance ask the adviser to reopen the case. He read out the offence again and immediately the prosecutor stood up and said 'I am offering no evidence'. I said 'Case dismissed. You are free to go' and he left the court with the usher who explained to him what had happened.

This was the nearest thing to a perverse verdict I can recall but we all thought that justice had been done. There was no suggestion of reasonable doubt (he was technically guilty) but we didn't want him to lose his job. It is noteworthy, however, that in each of the above cases the legal adviser was 'in cahoots' with the justices, and the prosecutor found the perfect solution.

After sitting in court for several years things were not becoming clearer, they were becoming more blurred. As a scientist I had hoped — and expected — the proceedings to be exact, like science. Of course, science is not exact but the degree of inexactitude can be measured. But the legal proceedings were not only inexact but based on a number of poorly understood abstractions. I was able by now in my mind to shed some of these. I was no longer concerned with innocence; I did not try to measure the reasonableness of any doubt I had: if I didn't think the defendant was guilty that is what I said. I was not concerned with scintillas. The professionals in the courtroom had probably reached the same conclusions that I had years earlier, but had realised that the best way to continue was to participate in the proceedings as if the abstractions really did exist: that there was such a thing as justice in the real world, 'reasonable doubt' meant the same thing to everybody, and that witnesses' recall was always accurate.

The years rolled on; new laws were enacted and new crimes were committed. A steady stream of defendants passed through the court. Everybody involved swore or affirmed that they would tell the truth and then in a significant number of cases proceeded to tell lies. What became increasingly apparent was that most of the defendants were not evil, were not professional criminals, and their offences were mainly trivial: motoring, shoplifting, bus fare avoidance, lacking a TV licence and the occasional crimes of violence or burglary. The most common serious offences were driving with excess alcohol, using a mobile phone whilst driving, and those involving Class A drugs. And most of the defendants were guilty, poor and struggling.

It became clear that although there might be justice (whatever that was) in the courtroom there was little justice in the world outside. The court in which I sat was in a poor area of London with a very mixed population; many were perpetually hard up, trying to make ends meet and mostly failing to do so.

Being a magistrate does not take up a great deal of time, roughly a half day a week. Apart from those in work, though, a fair number of JPs are retired and their remaining waking hours are devoted to leisure. My main leisure activities were—and are—reading, the theatre, watching some television programmes and swimming. Swimming is the odd one out as it does not involve crime or justice, but the visual arts do. The more I read, visited the theatre or the cinema or saw TV crime programmes the more interesting it became to watch how they depart from reality. Some works of fiction stick very closely to how the criminal justice system operates in real life, but many do not. The chapters that follow select and discuss a variety of films, books and plays; indicate how some of the problems associated with the conceptual nature of legal terminology are totally ignored and ask—and possibly answer—the question 'Does it matter?'

Part 1

THE POLICE

CHAPTER 1

Uniformed Police

In 1829 the first Metropolitan Police Act was passed and the Metropolitan Police Force was established when Sir Robert Peel was Home Secretary; police were colloquially known as 'Peelers' or 'Bobbies' but only the latter has stuck, possibly because the often used term 'British bobby' is alliterative. Before the police were launched their work was largely covered in London (except for the City) by the local watch. There were also other police forces within the metropolitan district outside the control of the Metropolitan Police District. By 1839 all these separate establishments were absorbed by the Metropolitan Police Force with the exception of the City of London Police which remains independent to this day.

The aims and objects of the new police were clearly set out by the Commissioners Rowan and Mayne:

'The primary object of an efficient police is the prevention of crime: the next that of detection and punishment of offenders if crime is committed. To these ends all efforts of the police must be directed. The protection of life and property, the preservation of public tranquillity, and the absence of crime will alone prove whether these efforts have been successful and whether the objects for which the police were appointed have been maintained.'

These are stringent standards; it is doubtful if they were ever successful; it is doubtful if they ever could be; they certainly are not today.

In *Twelfth Night* Viola comments,

> He must observe their mood on whom he jests
> The quality of person, and the time
> Not, like the haggard, check on every feather
> That comes before the eye. This is a practice
> As full of labour as a wise man's art...

She was not commenting on the British bobby but on Feste the Fool. It would appear then that the attributes of a good policeman match those of a good fool; this is hardly surprising if one recalls that Shakespeare's fools were 'licensed'; they could act with impunity in ways that for others would bring swift retribution from the court. But Shakespeare's fools knew what they were meant to be doing whereas today's police do not understand what their function really is. The perceived primary function of the modern British police is still crime prevention and detection, yet to these ends very little effort of the police is directed. Like the All England Croquet Club now famous for its tennis, the police force has developed into a fully mobile social service which, however, often embraces social and domestic disputes that may engender criminal offences.

Legitimacy of force

It is assumed that the occasional use of force is essential to keep order in society. The common law rules on justifiable force have been replaced by the Criminal Law Act 1967 which provides that *any person* can use such force as is reasonable in the circumstances in the prevention of crime, in effecting, or assisting in the lawful arrest of offenders or suspected offenders, or of persons unlawfully at large (Section 2(6)). Here we have another instance of the term 'reasonable'; not doubt this time, but circumstances. What is reasonable force? Depends on the circumstances. Catch a burglar in your house and immobilise him with a blow to the leg with a cricket bat and call the police: most people would call that reasonable. But smashing his head in with the same bat would be deemed excessive rather than reasonable and might result in a murder charge.

But although an ordinary citizen can use reasonable force in the circumstances above, what he cannot do which the police can, is to use their powers of arrest, which gives them greater scope for using legitimate force. In an attempt to clarify, the Royal Commission on Criminal Procedure (1981) said that the use of the term 'reasonable force' does not mean they can rely on force or the threat of force in the performance of their duties. But this is precisely what they do. Force, sometimes implied but explicit if necessary, is the kernel of the policeman's or police woman's power to exercise his or her authority. But whereas in 1981 they had the truncheon, now they have the

Taser and the gun, rubber and plastic bullets, water cannon and CS gas. In some circumstances 'minimal' can equal 'maximal', 'reasonable force' becomes 'overwhelming force' and 'acceptable' can mean anything. A few years later the Police and Criminal Evidence Act 1984 (known as PACE) gave the police authority to use force in no fewer than seventeen sections of the Act.

In the second decade of the 21st-century few would disagree that force remains the ultimate sanction in human affairs. As we shall see, few fictional representations of the police in action avoid violence.

The policeman's role

Although crime control may not be the main function of the police, it is, however, the core of their activities even if it does not take up most of their time. The criminal justice process is nearly always set in motion by the police. Policemen believe that real police work involves action: speeding to an emergency call, having a scuffle with a suspect, driving fast. The police emphasise their crime-fighting function and this image is influenced by many of the media. If emergencies are the cake of police work then the use of force is the icing.

Actual police work has been analysed in terms of peace keeping and as a social service. Analysing calls from the public in terms of 'law enforcement' or 'service' it has been found that service calls outnumbered law enforcement calls substantially in towns and overwhelmingly in the country. Order maintenance comprises most of police work and behind this capacity is the ability to use force lawfully. Thus although conflicts can be resolved without the police using their legal powers, the latent threat of their use is vital. Law enforcement occurs only when the police officer actually invokes his or her powers. Thus many of the services that the police perform depend on their ability to use force if needed and those services in which force is never needed could be done equally well by anybody else.

Police are called upon to act as social workers, vets, mental welfare officers, marriage counsellors, accommodation and child welfare officers, home help and by helping the infirm and confidantes.

The police are unique in claiming as their main function that which they do least (crime control), whilst denying the function that they perform best (service); and for failing to solve or prevent crime despite the use of an impressive battery of technological resources, yet keeping the peace and serving the public using few powers beyond those available to the ordinary citizen.

It is curious that not only are the police regarded differently by the public and by the police themselves but that neither viewpoint is in accord with reality. The police spend relatively little time fighting crime and have little claim to success. They deprecate their role as a social service, yet in many ways they are far superior to the conventional social services. The public regard them as crime fighters whilst using them overwhelmingly in their social service capacity.

It is hardly surprising that the written and performing media do not devote their efforts to storylines involving police officers rescuing cats from trees or calming arguments between husbands and wives. As we shall see, police in fiction are romanticised either as the gutsy and violent 'Sweeney' (Todd: Flying Squad) or the docile Dixon of Dock Green, the archetype friendly local copper. There are no TV programmes or films about a police officer who directs the flow of traffic.

However, it is important that the police are to some extent glorified in a role they only erratically fulfil. There would be little public confidence if it became evident that they spent their time wandering the streets and stumbling across a crime every few years. It is equally important that the police see themselves as macho crime fighters; and if it were acknowledged that the powers vested in them are used to serve the public in an infinite diversity of situations, they would attract few recruits.

The uniformed police are like cats. For most of the time they keep their claws retracted and rarely use them. They enjoy a chase but rarely catch anything. They provide comfort for old ladies and children who know nothing of claws. But when they go out for a stroll the mice are very, very careful.

CHAPTER 2

Detectives

The police are divided into two main sections. One section, described above, keeps the peace, walks the streets, patrols in police cars and on motor cycles, deters crime, catches criminals in the act of committing and shortly after they have committed an offence, and provides a variety of social services. The other section attempts, sometimes successfully, to catch criminals who have committed an offence and have left the scene of the crime. Police in the first section wear police uniform when they are on duty (although they have the same powers and authority when they are off-duty and are not wearing uniform) and are known as uniformed police officers; the detectives do not wear uniform (except for formal occasions) and are known as plain clothes police. Their functions do not include any of the sociological functions that are performed by the uniformed police. All police carry formal identification called warrant cards which are produced on demand, particularly by plain clothes police who have no other means of demonstrating that they are police officers. Uniformed police are addressed by their rank: constable, inspector, etc; plain clothes police have the prefix 'detective' and are: detective constable, detective chief superintendent, etc.

There are also a large number of people employed by the police who have nothing directly to do with police work. They are 'civilians' who may be typists, run the canteens, medical examiners, forensic scientists and others (even though some of these functions may nowadays be outsourced).

When a person is caught at the scene of a crime, as happens when stopped by the police for speeding or not having a car properly insured, or for shoplifting for example, the matter is dealt with by uniformed police who may be on the spot (roads) or called in (shops). For relatively minor offences such as those above the officer will take down the details of the offender, the location of the offence and where appropriate, statements from any witnesses, or from the offender. At this stage the offender is not obliged to say anything and can, if he or she chooses, walk away but if he she does so may be arrested. In the fullness of time the offender will receive a notice instructing him when to attend a magistrates' court in the area where the offence took place. If the offender pleads or is found guilty he or she will usually be fined; if the offence is more serious a trial may be deferred to a later date in order that a case can be made and witnesses ordered to attend. If he or she is arrested they must be cautioned. The caution is read out and explains that the offender still does not have to say anything but if he or she fails to say anything that they later rely on in court it may count against them. Once someone is cautioned he is taken to the police station where he or she may make a statement or be interrogated or both. Depending on what the offender says or what the officers have observed, he or she may be charged with a specific offence or released. If charged, he or she will be tried in a magistrates' court unless the offence is serious when the case will be sent to (and he or she will be committed for to a trial at) the Crown Court before a judge and jury.

Uniformed police officers on the street usually work in pairs, rarely alone. Those who work in the police station have separate duties, and although they co-operate, they mostly work alone.

Detectives mostly work in teams. Teams are led by a senior officer, usually a detective inspector or a detective chief inspector, the rest of the team often comprising a detective sergeant and possibly one or more detective constables. Detectives often work with others, such as scene of crime officers, forensic experts, medical experts and pathologists. They rarely work alone but rely on a large measure of support from within and outside the police. They are concerned exclusively with crime; they provide no direct services to the public.

CHAPTER 3

The Police in Fiction

Literature

Although in the United States of America there are writers whose crime novels show how police forces operate—the novels of Ed McBain which are set firmly in the New York Police Department are a good example—early crime fiction on both sides of the Atlantic relied on a single detective operating alone, whether a police officer, an amateur detective with a knack for solving crimes, or a private detective. In this regard most crime fiction, particularly British, departs from what goes on in a real police force.

Although there are a few other contenders it is generally considered that the first detective story published was *The Murders in the Rue Morgue* by Edgar Allan Poe. It is a short story and appeared in *Graham's Magazine* in 1841. The Rue Morgue is a fictional street in Paris and is in the 'closed room'-style of crime fiction where two women were brutally murdered in a room which seemed to offer no means of entrance or of exit. The murders are solved by one C Auguste Dupin, who was not a detective but worked out by rational thought how the murders were carried out, a process which Poe called 'ratiocination'. Dupin appears as the mystery solver in two further short stories. Films were made of the story in 1932 and 1971.

Poe's tales had clever plots that intrigued readers; he wrote well but he was not an engaging character. He had had a poor start and a short and tragic life. His father left the family early and his mother died when he was three. He began writing at an early age, mainly poetry, and lived with his aunt and uncle. He went to the University of West Virginia, got into debt, tried to pay his debts by gambling and failed, and left. He joined the army and went to the West Point Academy. Although he was good at his studies he neglected his duties and was kicked out. In 1836 he married his thirteen-year-old cousin Virginia; she died of tuberculosis three years later. Although he became a gambler and an alcoholic he never stopped writing. He died in 1849 at the age of forty.

Being the first crime fiction writer, Poe could not have known that he had set the pattern for this genre: an intriguing crime — usually murder — solved by a clever individual who was not a policeman.

The accolade of being the first author to write a full length crime novel goes virtually unopposed to William Wilkie Collins who was born in 1824. The novel is *The Moonstone*, published in 1868. He had written a number of novels earlier but in one decade he wrote the four novels for which he is largely remembered: *The Woman in White* (1860), *No Name* (1862), *Armadale* (1866) and *The Moonstone* (1868).

Unlike Edgar Allan Poe, Collins was born into a well-off family and had a good education; he studied law at Lincoln's Inn and was called to the bar but he never practised law. Like Poe, in some respects he was something of a rake; he led a bohemian lifestyle, drank wine excessively and was an opium user. He had relationships with two women, lived with one of them but married neither. But even after the publication of *The Moonstone* he continued to write prodigiously and died in 1889.

The plot of *The Moonstone* is complex. The gem is a yellow diamond which is the centrepiece of the Hindu sacred god of the moon. One John Hardcastle, who is with the British army in India, kills the three men guarding the stone, steals it and takes it back to England. He then wills the stone to his niece Rachel, who is given it by Franklyn Blake with whom Rachel is in love, and she wears it at a dinner party for her birthday. She leaves it in her sitting room overnight and it is gone in the morning. The local police are called and Superintendent Seegrave arrives but proves inept. Franklyn then calls for Sergeant Cuff of London to take over the investigation of the missing diamond. The narrative of the story is told by several people successively but in the end Sergeant Cuff locates the stone and restores it to Rachel. It is a very clever and intricate plot, but again bears little relation to how the police worked even in the mid-19th-century. Cuff, who is a police officer of low rank, works alone and solves the mystery, locates and restores the moonstone which is returned not to Rachel but to the Hindus in India. As a bonus Rachel and Franklyn are engaged to be married at the end of the book. So intricate is the plot that the reader is at a complete loss as to how it will be unravelled and solved but Cuff manages to do it virtually by himself.

It is this novel that sets the format for a police officer who works alone even though he is employed by a police force, and like many of the novels and short stories that follow, shows how he or she not only defeats the criminal but in doing so outwits his or her fellow and senior officers; which is not how the police operate.

The stories and novels of Sir Arthur Conan Doyle are a milestone in crime writing and his main character is recognised in almost every country in the world. Sherlock Holmes is not a policeman at all; he is a private detective working alone with his assistant Dr John Watson. The solution to his mysteries are arrived at by the same method employed by Edgar Allan Poe: ratiocination.

Arthur Conan Doyle was Arthur Ignatius Conan Doyle where 'Conan' was probably another middle name which he adopted as part of his surname. He was born in 1859 in Edinburgh to a poor family with an alcoholic father. He was Charles and Mary Doyle's second child and had an elder sister and five other siblings. Due to his father's alcoholism the family were split up but came together again in 1867 in a squalid flat. Thanks to his wealthy uncles he was educated in some top schools and between 1875 and 1876 he attended a Jesuit school in Feldkirch, Austria which is not far from the Reichenbach Falls where he was to set one of his most dramatic incidents.

From 1876 to 1881 he was a student at the University of Edinburgh Medical School. It was here that Conan Doyle met Dr Joseph Bell whom he claimed to be the most notable character he had met. Bell was a surgeon at Edinburgh Infirmary and he had remarkable powers of observation and of deductions from these observations. He was not only able by these means to arrive at a diagnosis but also to work out the patient's job and lifestyle. He took Conan Doyle on as a ward assistant where the latter learned his methods: look at the face, the colouring, the clothes, the hands, the shoes—and from all these data deducing what it was needed to know. This was the model for the most famous fictional detective in the world.

Whilst still a student he published his first story *The Mystery of Sasassa Valley* about a treasure hunt set in South Africa. It leaned heavily on Poe's style; he considered Poe to be 'the supreme original story writer of all time'. If you are the first, of course, you must be original; and 'all time' was but a few decades; and apart from Wilkie Collins and himself there was little competition. This is not to diminish Poe, for his originality has not faded over the years and his *Tales of Mystery and Imagination* are very clever: mysterious and imaginative.

After Conan Doyle qualified, he set up a medical practice with an ex-classmate in Plymouth but the relationship failed and Conan Doyle moved to Portsmouth where he set up alone in Southsea. The practice was not a success which left him plenty of time to write stories and his first novels.

The fifty-six short stories and four novels featuring Sherlock Holmes spanned forty years from 1887. He also wrote twenty-one other novels, more than 150 short stories, non-fiction, and three volumes of poetry. Holmes was a brilliant deductive private detective who was introduced with his assistant Dr Watson at 221b Baker Street in London in a novel called *A Study in Scarlet* in 1887. His method of solving crimes was by means of pure deduction preceded by intense and detailed observation; for his time he used whatever science and technology was available to solve cases that seemed unsolvable and for which his clients must have paid large fees to allow a fairly lavish lifestyle. He solved crimes that the police failed to solve and those which the clients brought straight to Holmes, bypassing the police altogether.

Unlike his creation who had a laser-like mind, Conan Doyle was something of a polymath and a sportsman. Apart from his wide range of writing he played football for an early Portsmouth team, as goalkeeper, and also played cricket for the MCC mainly as a batsman but occasionally as a bowler, but took only one wicket ever: that of the legendary cricketer W G Grace.

The methods used by Sherlock Holmes were quite remote from those employed by the police, and in the stories he was always ultimately successful. But although his methods were unrealistic and audacious he was and is the greatest fictional detective of them all.

Before leaving Conan Doyle and his detective it is worth noting that he was very interested in justice and injustice. His interventions led to two accused men being exonerated. One of them, George Edalji, was featured in the novel *Arthur and George* by Julian Barnes (2005) and his interventions led to the Court of Criminal Appeal being set up in 1907.

Although known authors of detective stories were exclusively male until 1914, from 1915 onwards there have been a substantial number of female writers. Nevertheless, whether written by men or women, fictional detectives are overwhelmingly male.

However, two of the most prolific of detective writers spanning much of the last century were women: Dorothy L Sayers and Agatha Christie. They each had a male detective who was not a policeman, continuing the genre started by Poe many years earlier.

Dorothy Leigh Sayers was born in 1893 and although she died in 1957 of a heart attack some of her books continued to be published after her death, the last one, *The Travelling Rug* as late as 2005.

Her first book *Whose Body?* appeared in 1923 so her writing career spanned thirty four years. Her detective was the rather eccentric Lord Peter Wimsey. Although he was in the same mould as his predecessors as a solitary figure solving crimes for his own amusement, he had a friend who had been a sergeant at Scotland Yard who rose to the rank of commander. Much later, another woman crime writer chose her solitary detective, Adam Galbraith, to be an actual policeman who also rises to commander but who solves crimes almost on his own with a little help from his underlings. Wimsey was very rich, a bon viveur, an athlete and unlike many fictional detectives had a family. But like his fictional predecessors he works alone, is not a policeman and uses none of the painstaking detective work associated with the police.

Sayer's contemporary Agatha Christie, who was born in 1890 and died in 1976, was even more prolific and invented two detectives—one a woman—who appeared in separate stories, never together.

Miss (Jane) Marple appeared in twelve novels and twenty short stories. Elderly and unmarried, she lived a simple life in the fictional village of St Mary Mead. She, too, had a police connection, a retired commissioner of the Metropolitan Police, no less, from whom she gleans information; but he was never involved in her solving crimes, nearly always murders.

Miss Marple was of independent means and had never worked; a genteel busybody fond of knitting and gardening, and particularly gossiping where she picked up titbits of information which her shrewdness and intelligence enabled her to piece together to solve crimes. She had a rather cynical view of humanity and was quite unpleasant and shrew-like in her first short story, *The Thirteen Problems* which was serialised in *Sketch* magazine in 1927, but in the later works became refined and mannerly, always ready to exchange the time of day in apparently idle chatter with other villagers. It was her amiable gossiping that enabled her to solve the mysteries by piecing together the scraps of information she thus picked up.

Christie's male detective first appeared in her first crime novel *The Mysterious Affair at Styles* in 1920. His appearance spanned more than half a century, his last appearance, in *Curtain,* being in 1975.

Hercule Poirot was more of a caricature than a character. He was a Belgian who had settled in England to lead a quiet life growing marrows. Little more that five feet three, he was rotund, slightly balding with a round face and an impeccably styled moustache. His clothing was very conservative and meticulously cared for, in particular his patent leather shoes. In short, he was a quaint dandy. He spoke good English with a strong Belgian (or French) accent peppered with French phrases and words and was scrupulously polite. It is hardly surprising that in 1930 she found her brainchild 'insufferable' and thirty years later described him as an 'ego-centric little creep'; but failed to kill off her loved-by-the-public golden goose.

Whereas Miss Marple solved her mysteries by herself Poirot had an assistant called Hastings, who was more of a stooge than a help, with whom Poirot could try out his theories. Hastings was probably based on Holmes' friend Dr Watson but was not nearly so clever. He was also given an 'aunt Sally' in the form of one Inspector Japp, a Scotland Yard detective who was constantly bettered by Poirot and whom Poirot frequently mocks as a rival and is dismissive of his following a traditional trail of clues.

Poirot differs from Miss Marples in another way too. Whereas she gradually and carefully gathers together various scraps of knowledge which she pieces together to identify the killer, Poirot's methods are more psychological, focussing on the background and nature of the victim and attempting to determine the type of criminal who would commit the crime; certain types of crimes are committed by certain types of people. Poirot is a more direct descendant of Poe; Poe's 'ratiocination' is translated into Poirot's reliance on his 'little grey cells'. He spends far more time thinking about the crime, the criminal and the victim than he spends looking for clues.

Arthur Conan Doyle hailed Edgar Allan Poe as a great crime writer and emulated his hero, a single amateur detective who solved crimes by ratiocination. He acknowledged that he based his detective on Poe's C Auguste Dupin, and gave Sherlock Holmes his mentor Joseph Bell's talents. Conan Doyle's hero was a super-sleuth with extra-ordinary powers of observation and in particular, deduction. Lord Peter Wimsey was another eccentric working alone to solve crimes. Miss Marple, the first female detective, was more of an information-gatherer and in her inimitable casual way identified murderers. And Agatha Christie, possibly the greatest crime writer in more than a century, admitted that she was writing in the Sherlock Holmes mould with an eccentric detective, a stooge assistant and a Scotland Yard detective, Inspector Yapp, bettered by Poirot at every turn.

Although many crime writers invented their own detective who worked alone with little if any contact with the police whom they invariably bettered in the nicest possible way, there were some writers who sometimes went out of their way—indeed, it seemed this was the whole purpose of the plot—to make the police officer look stupid. One such is *The Scarlet Butterfly* by Dulcie Gray. The story, which is very short, consists largely of a conversation between the suspect, known only as Verney, and the superintendent in charge of the case. The dead woman, Lydia, had rejected Verney's offer of marriage twenty five years earlier in favour of Bobby who had been killed in a car crash years later. Other characters were Vincent, Lydia's step-son, a 'vicious playboy' who was in line to inherit Lydia's house and money; and Clara, her daughter who hated her for breaking up an earlier romance. There was also Colonel Lethbridge to whom Lydia had written some passionate love letters after Bobby's death for which he was blackmailing her. The butterfly brooch of the title was in the hair of the dead Lydia. The case against Verney, as outlined gradually by the superintendent, seems strong: all Verney's alibis are countered. And then, with less than a page to go, Verney recalls an incident the previous summer when he had received a phone call from Clara inviting herself to dinner. After the meal he had had to see her home and furthermore, into her bedroom. He rejected her advances and told her she was infinitely less attractive than her mother. He concludes that she had framed him. He tells the superintendent to search Clara's room where he would find clues leading to her guilt. At this point there is a commotion outside and when the door is opened there is Clara. She tells the superintendent he is too late, she has swallowed cyanide and falls down dead. If Ms Gray's aim was to show the superintendent and by extension the police in a poor light she succeeded, but only by their departing totally from real life police officers.

(Enoch) Arnold Bennett 1869-1931, is best known for his novels about the Five Towns that were later subsumed into Stoke-on-Trent. However, he wrote at least one crime short story, *Murder!*, published in 1926, in which the reader knows whodunit, the police officer works out what happened but does not know who did it, a non-police amateur detective tells the superintendent how the crime was committed and by whom. And they are all wrong.

Two acquaintances, Lomax Harder and John Franting are connected by the fact that Harder is in love with Franting's wife Emily and she with him. Franting is aware of this, does not love Emily but does not want Harder or anyone else to have her. He is also aware that Emily has booked a passage from Harwich to Copenhagen, a city where Harder has interests and visits often. Before the actual story opens there is a short paragraph with Bennett musing about murder: two a week in England and two hundred in the USA, not counting deaths where murder is not suspected, and that some forty per cent of murderers are never caught and they move safely among us. Such is life, he concludes, such is homicide.

The two men are in the fictional seaside town of Quangate and Franting enters a gunsmith's in order to buy a revolver. He chooses a Webley Mark III and while he is at the range to try it out Harder picks up another to look at and idly slips it into his pocket. Franting, though complaining that he had had only one practice shot, buys the gun and Harder follows him back to his hotel and following Franter still, finds himself in a billiard room built within a courtyard. They argue about Emily and Franting pulls out a letter from her indicating that she is leaving him and tells Harder that if she does he will kill her. He tears the letter in half and drops it in the grate. Harder knew he meant it and being devoted to her takes the revolver from his pocket and fires a single shot at Franting, killing him. He puts on gloves and makes his exit via the window into the courtyard and away. He walked along the seafront and after dropping his gun into the harbour, he took a train to London, then another to Harwich, caught the boat to Copenhagen where he sought out and found Emily to their joint delight.

Meanwhile, a superintendent and his sergeant are in the billiard room examining evidence when a famous private detective, Dr Bond, renowned for having solved famous mysteries, arrives to the chagrin of the superintendent. Bond examined the body and stated he had been dead for ninety minutes and was told that it was found by the woman who came in to make up the fire. The superintendent proudly displayed fingerprints on the window frame using a torch, and footprints on the sill with some strands of blue cloth. He explained that the killer must have been tall from the angle of fire, and he wore a blue suit which had been slightly torn. One of his boots had a hole and he had only three fingers on one hand. He deduced that he had entered and left by the window. After interviewing the porter who lied by saying that nobody had entered the hotel via the lobby, the amateur detective proceeded to destroy the superintendent's solution by interviewing the charwoman. He noticed that she was missing a finger on one hand (a mangle accident) and established that she had cleaned the window that morning. Her left boot had a hole and her skirt was torn at the hem.

The detective, Dr Bond, apologised for destroying the superintendent's evidence and explained that he had seen the charwoman earlier and had noticed the missing finger. He felt sure that no-one had entered or left through the window and that Franting had shot himself. When the superintendent asked where he had hidden the gun after he was dead, Bond pointed to the bulge in his overcoat. The policeman withdrew a Webley Mark III which had recently fired one shot and had fallen into his pocket. Dr Bond explained that Franting could not bear the thought that Emily was leaving him and shot himself, the gun falling from his hand into his pocket. He retrieved the unburnt part of the letter from the grate and read the end of it: '... you have killed my affection for you, and I shall leave our home tomorrow. This is absolutely final. E.'

Bond leaves, having demonstrated that police-officers are a set of numb-skulls. The tale ends with Harder and Emily in Copenhagen reading in an English paper that at Franting's inquest the jury returned a verdict of suicide.

This is a very cleverly crafted story with great attention to detail; all the facts fit both the superintendent's and Dr Bond's explanation of what actually happened, each version quite different from the other, and neither of them correct. Arnold Bennett is having a laugh at the police, at clever-dick amateur detectives, and also at detective stories, and to do that in the genre he is ridiculing took a lot of skill. It also took a lot of foresight. *Murder!* was written in 1926; the first Miss Marple story appeared in 1927; the first Allingham/Campion story (see later) appeared in 1929. If Bennett was having a laugh it must have been at the expense of Sherlock Holmes and Hercule

Poirot who saw the light of day in 1920.

Thus each successive and overlapping crime writer copied the format of a predecessor going back to Poe. It is hardly surprising, then, that the detective in all these tales was an amateur who worked alone and who had no formal relations with the police. All were eccentric in different ways and all were invariably successful. The quality of their writing was not the same; arguably Wilkie Collins was the best stylist and Agatha Christie the poorest, but made up for this deficiency by writing the cleverest plots.

The earlier decades of the twentieth century was a good time for writers, particularly women writers who were mostly all contemporaries of each other. Margery Allingham who was born in 1904 and died in 1966, came from a family who wrote, as did many of her parents' friends. Her first novel, *Blackkerchief Dick* came out in 1923 when she was only 19 and she was not slow to point out that Agatha Christie was already 30 when her first book was published. Her first detective story was serialised in the *Daily Express* in 1927 under the title of *The White Cottage Mystery* but her breakthrough came with her 1929 novel *The Crime at Black Dudley* which introduced her own detective to the scene: Albert Campion. Campion was an unlikely detective with protruding teeth and a falsetto voice, a 'fresh-faced young man with the tow coloured hair and his foolish pale blue eyes behind tortoise-rimmed spectacles'. He, like Peter Wimsey, came from an aristocratic background. The next book a year later gave him an assistant, one Magersfontein Lugg. Campion worked throughout the thirties and into the war when he was employed as an agent. After the war the reading public demanded more realism and Albert Campion gradually changed from a compulsive giggler into a more serious and mature character.

Book followed book throughout the next two decades until Allingham was stricken with breast cancer and died in 1966. Her detective and his mate were strikingly different from those that had come before but their *modus operandi* was the same: working alone with no contact with the police.

P D (Phyllis Dorothy) James was born in 1920 and Ruth (Barbara) Rendall a decade later. Both have been elevated to the House of Lords; James sat as a Conservative and Rendall is a Labour peer. Both are known more for their crime fiction than for their politics.

They each began writing detective fiction in the 1960s. James had a number of jobs in government departments such as the National Health Service and when her husband died two years after the publication of her first crime novel she became a civil servant at the Home Office. She was briefly a magistrate but had to retire when she became a baroness.

P D James' detective is an actual police officer who works in London from New Scotland Yard. The first novel in which Chief Inspector Adam Dalgliesh appeared, in 1962, was *Cover Her Face*. Fourteen books later, the last Dalgliesh book, by which time he has risen to the rank of Commander in charge of the Special Investigations Squad, is called *The Private Patient*. Published in 2008, it is the last in which he will appear. Unlike most fictional detectives Dalgliesh is rather remote and ascetic. He lives alone since his wife died, writes and publishes poetry, and although he is in charge of other officers he tends to solve the mysteries himself. Being intellectual and introspective he employs the ratiocination method of crime solving first introduced by Poe's C Auguste Dupin.

Ruth Rendall's detective, Chief Inspector Wexford, is not at all like Dalgliesh. When he was introduced in 1964 in *From Doon With Death* he was already fifty two years old and somewhat ugly. He is a family man with a wife in a wheelchair and two daughters, one on the stage, and lives and works in a small town in Sussex. He is closer to a real police detective than any of those previously described, is in and out of his police station and he heads a small team of detectives. So far there have been twenty four Wexford books, the latest, published in 2013 being *No Man's Nightingale*. An example of Rendall's style can be seen in *The Babes in the Wood* published in 2003. Wexford and his family are not a day older but the events do not necessarily take place close to the date of publication. The story concerns the disappearance of two teenage siblings and their weekend sitter, a woman in her early thirties. Although Wexford is the central detective he works from a real police station in the fictional Sussex town of Kingsmarkham and is assisted by an inspector, a detective sergeant and various constables including a couple of female officers who all have a useful input. When necessary he is also in touch with other local services and does not shrink from seeking the help of other constabularies.

Writing under the pseudonym of Barbara Vine, Rendall has written other mystery novels, often of a deeper nature than those involving Wexford. The first Vine book, *A Dark Adapted Eye*, was published in 1986 and the latest, *The Child's Child*, in 2012.

During what is called the Golden Age of crime fiction, from 1915 to about 1945, female writers dominated and their proportion increased. After the end of the war female writers became fewer and male writers were on the increase. However, during the time of female dominance male writers did exist and possibly the best of them was Michael Innes.

Michael Innes was the pen name of John Innes Macintosh Stewart and he lived between 1906 and 1994. Apart from writing more than fifty crime novels and short story collections he had a very successful academic career, working at a number of universities in Britain, Australia and the USA as a teacher and sometime professor of English language.

His first book *Death at the President's Lodging* came out in 1936 and featured Inspector John Appleby, a poorly educated but intellectually curious and intelligent policeman. Appleby returns in Innes' second book, *Hamlet, Revenge* and after retiring as an inspector, five years later returns as Sir John Appleby, Assistant Commissioner of the Met.

If the quality of Agatha Christie's literary style (but not her plotting) has been called into question, Innes' writing is elegant as becomes a teacher of English. He is very much a stylist as this extract from *Hamlet, Revenge* demonstrates:

> The mid-summer dusk is deepening on Horton Hill. The sheep are shadowy on its slopes; to the north the softly-rolling downland is sharpening into silhouette; and below, Scamnum is grown mysterious...The spirits sinister and ironic look down on Scamnum Court these nights.

A foretaste of Dylan Thomas.

Hamlet, Revenge concerns a murder that takes place during an amateur performance of Hamlet at the country home, Scamnum Court, of the Duke of Norton. The victim is none other than Lord Aldearn the Lord Chancellor of England. There are many characters in the book as might be expected with a large audience and the cast of Hamlet. When the victim's body is found soon after he is shot the Duke contacts the Prime Minister who gets in touch with the Commissioner of the Metropolitan Police. From all the detectives in the Met the commissioner selects Inspector Appleby even above Appleby's superior, a superintendent. Appleby and a sergeant are driven down to Scamnum Hall in Sussex and there any resemblance between the inspector and the real police disappears. Although Appleby is a fine detective, and nothing like the eccentric Lord Peter Wimsey or Campion, he works alone with his sergeant's help and notwithstanding there is a further murder, solves both.

So complex is the plot and so intricate is Appleby's investigation and interpretation of events that the denouement, or denouements for there are two, take up almost half the book. And Innes, in the midst of the intellectual swordplay, cannot resist a little joke:

Mrs Platt-Hunter-Platt says,

'And in my opinion the Duke should send for a detective.'

'A detective' said Noel politely from across the table. 'You mean a real detective, not like the police?' 'Exactly—a real detective. There is a very good man whose name I forget; a foreigner and very conceited—but, they say, thoroughly reliable.'

A dig at the police and a compliment to Agatha Christie and Poirot.

The first Inspector Morse book, *Last Bus to Woodstock*, was written in 1975 by (Norman) Colin Dexter who was born in 1930. There were thirteen Morse books, the last one being *The Remorseful Day*, published in 1999. Although the books had a large readership, Inspector Morse really came into his own when the stories were presented as crime drama on television with John Thaw playing Morse and Kevin Whatley as his side-kick, Sergeant Lewis. In some ways Morse resembles Galbraith, P D James' copper: he is very intellectual, introspective, unmarried, a lover of classical music especially opera, and a devotee of crossword puzzles and beer. Lewis is his butt and although Morse—his first name was revealed very late as Endeavour—was sometimes quite rude to him, it was often Lewis who had the flash of inspiration that led to the criminal being caught.

As to the rest of the police in Oxford, where Morse operates, there are occasional episodes where uniformed officers help with the donkey work, and brushes with the chief superintendent who is Morse's superior, but Morse and Lewis work together, virtually alone.

Reginald (Charles) Hill (1936–2012), one of the best modern crime writers, wrote jokes, amusing scenes and a substantial number of novels, but it is his crime novels, featuring Dalziel and Pascoe for which he is well known. Hill had a degree in English which he uses to advantage, peppering his pages with literary flourishes and obscure words. There are also many jokes and funny episodes. His two detectives were introduced in *A Clubbable Woman* in 1970 and bowed out in 2009 with *Midnight Fugue;* between those dates twenty four Dalziel and Pascoe novels as well as a number of short stories under the title of *There Are No Ghosts in the Soviet Union* published in 2000. He also wrote a number of books featuring a black private detective called Joe Sixsmith who operates in Luton, Bedfordshire. The Sixsmith books are quite different from the Dalzeal and Pascoe stories which mostly take place in Yorkshire, being droll rather than hilarious, and having more social content from a leftish viewpoint.

Andrew Dalziel (pronounced Dee-ell), known to his intimates as Fat Andy, is unlike other detectives, fictional or otherwise. He is fat, boisterous and a lover of food, malt whiskey and well-developed women. He is totally unintellectual and may even be anti-intellectual, but with a sharp mind. Throughout all the novels Dalziel remains a detective superintendent. His assistant, Peter Pascoe who in the early novels is a detective sergeant and later becomes a detective inspector then a detective chief inspector, is university educated and somewhat pedantic. He is married to the astute and often acerbic Ellie and has a precocious young daughter called Rosie. Ellie is very liberal and often clashes with Dalziel but they have a soft spot for each other and when in *The Death of Dalziel* she believes that he has died from a gunshot she is overwrought with grief. In the later novels, Pascoe and Ellie divorce and she and Rosie emigrate to the USA. One other character should be mentioned, Sergeant Edgar Wield, an extremely ugly, methodical and careful officer who plays by the book. He is gay and lives with his partner. Wield is a perfect foil for the other two: a plodder with flair.

Hill's plots are very clever but with the fascinating cast he has assembled the books would be readable even without the mysteries. Many of the stories are not in the traditional mould, but have a variable time line; some touch upon social issues; and Dalziel himself is quite unlike other fictional detectives.

In an interview Hill emphasised that his books were not about police procedurals, a detailed account of a detective's view of the investigation of a crime; he omits the humdrum work which takes up ninety per cent of a police officer's day. His characters are also different in that whereas the junior partners of the main detectives—Dr Watson, Sergeant Lewis—are less intelligent than the principal, Pascoe and Dalziel are intellectually the other way round.

In some ways these stories describe an environment closer to the real thing than in any previous detective novel. The buffoon and his educated assistant operate in a real police station in Yorkshire, go through fairly normal police procedures whilst leaving out the boring bits, and there is a substantial cast of other police officers, both men and women, who have 'walk on' roles. One book ends with one of the detectives being murdered by another police officer who is not even suspected. Even Innes' Inspector Appleby, though a police officer in the Met, behaves like a private detective little different from, say, Campion. It is not surprising that such a motley cast of diverse characters that Reginald Hill had conjured up should be converted into a television series; nor is it surprising that the TV rendition does not approach the subtlety, humour and literary dazzle of the books.

Sometimes crime writers for one reason or another known only to themselves stray off the beaten track, go off the rails, think outside the box, leave their comfort zone … and write a spoof. The great American short story writer O Henry, master of the twist in the tail, wrote some six hundred short stories most of which were not about crime but some were so ingenious and so amusing that they might be considered mild spoofs. For an example of a British crime writer one can turn to Ernest Bramah (Smith), 1868-1942, who wrote a number of shaggy dog detective stories which had a considerable following. But for an undeniable, uproarious spoof whose 'hero' is not a detective but an inept young doctor called John Humdrum one can turn to a tale written in the early part of the 20th-century called *Smothered in Corpses*. In the first paragraph the doctor opens his book cabinet to reveal the body of a man wearing evening dress 'of the most expensive cut'. He recalled that he had earlier been summoned by a lady in a 'magnificently appointed motor-car' who appealed to him 'in a marked Castilian accent' (which only an expert in the Spanish language would be likely to detect) to accompany her to the slums of Limehouse. There he meets a sick child who, he was informed by a Chinaman speaking pidgin English, had swallowed a button; his treatment was to recommend sending her to the nearest hospital.

While recalling this, his French windows burst open and a girl of ravishing beauty springs into the room and implores him to save her from her enemies. She then sweeps a corpse from the doctor's dissecting table and takes its place as Inspector Badger of the Detective Service enters to discuss the case of the murdered prima donna who had left Covent Garden at eleven thirty the previous night. Humdrum points out that that was late for shopping as the market would be closed at that time but Badger informs him that 'there is a sort of play-house there where a lot of these foreigners appear.'

A cast of crazy characters, some dead, some not, pass through the remaining pages; there is no plot, only bizarre and unexplained goings-on. The few thousand words of the story continue with the doctor stumbling across another corpse which 'needed no second glance' to establish that it was the mysterious Ethiopian minstrel who had greeted him as 'Uncle Sam' on Boat Race night. After delivering an urgent document to the Admiral of the Fleet at Plyhampton, which he reaches by changing taxis seventeen times. He is offered the post of Surgeon General of the Fleet but ends up with the Admiral's daughter. Humdrum says, 'Had we not better explain to them now, darling, exactly what it was all about' and she replies, 'No, dearest; I don't think we better had.' So we shall never know!

☙

Even from the tiny sample above of the thousands of detective novels and short stories published in Britain in the past hundred years it is clear that the fictional detectives bear little resemblance to real police officers. The fictional detectives are sometimes eccentric like Campion; sometimes more a caricature like Poirot; sometimes cerebral like Dalgliesh; sometimes oafish like Dalziel.

Although detective work is probably more interesting and less tedious than that of the uniformed branch there is still a great deal of painstaking investigation, interviewing of possible suspects, following up leads that lead nowhere and so on. Days and weeks of meticulous work is carried out often with nothing to show for it. Reginald Hill put his finger on the distinction between real and fictional detectives when he pointed out that the procedures that the police go through are extremely tedious and often fruitless; and would be unreadable. Fictional crime and its detection almost always involves a detective with at least flair (Dalziel) or even genius (Holmes) and the stories always conclude with the criminal being caught and brought to justice. Nobody would want to read about a stodgy detective working his way through a couple of hundred pages and failing to catch his man; nor would any author want to write such a piece.

Theatre

Compared with books and film and television there have been relatively few major professional plays in which the police play a major role. This is hardly surprising since although a crime mystery with a detective would be possible in a theatrical production, a play in which a number of policemen were involved would be difficult if not impossible. Certainly having a large number of police would be impossible on a stage.

Agatha Christie adapted one of her books, *The Hollow*, into a play which involved two police officers: the usual inspector (Colquhoun) and a sergeant (Penny). Buoyed by the relative success of this play she then proceeded to write a play from scratch, not based on one of her books. The play was *The Mousetrap* which was first performed in 1952 and is still running at St Martin's theatre in London and has been performed more than 25,000 times.

The format of the play is a traditional country house murder in the snowed-in Monkwell Manor. The entire play takes place in the Great Hall. It opens on a dark stage and by sound only the murder of a woman is played out. The action then moves to the manor which has recently been converted to a guest house by Mollie and Giles Ralston. Four guests arrive: Christopher Wren, Mrs Boyle, Major Metcalfe and Miss Casewell. Mrs Boyle is a nuisance and complains about everything but refuses Giles' offer to cancel her booking. Due to the severe snowfall they are virtually trapped and read of the London murder in the newspaper. A fifth guest arrives, Mr Paravicini, on foot, after running his car into a snowdrift.

Mrs Boyle continues to complain and the other guests try to keep away from her. Then the police call which causes alarm, and shortly after Sergeant Trotter arrives on skis, possibly the only English copper ever to have done so. He informs the group that he believes a murderer to be at large and is on his way to the guest house following the death of Maureen Lyon in London. Just how he would reach the guest house given the problem encountered by Mr Paravicini, and Sergeant Trotter's novel means of transport, does not seem to have occurred to any of the guests.

Mrs Boyle is killed and the other guests realize that the murderer is already among them as either one of the guests or their hosts. Sergeant Trotter assembles them with a plan to set a trap. The play builds to a climax with a twist ending in which it is revealed that Trotter himself is the murderer and that the Major is the real police officer who suspected Trotter from the outset when he claimed to be a police sergeant.

What is interesting is that although the plot of the play is complex and there is an intricate explanation leading to the outcome, with a bogus policeman who is hyperactive and a real policeman who does nothing, the usual format is followed. Not only is there nothing remotely real about the situation but the police are not involved except for Major Metcalf who is everything that a normal policeman is not.

J B (John Boynton) Priestly lived for 90 years between 1894 and 1984—what changes he must have seen— during which time he was a most prolific writer whose output included more than 120 books and over 50 plays. Of all his plays *An Inspector Calls* is considered by many his finest work for the stage. It was given its first performance in 1945 in the Soviet Union and was staged in Britain in the following year. Although superficially it has the *format* of a conventional murder mystery—indeed there is no murder—that is not its main purpose; it is really about class and responsibility and how responsibility to society is viewed by people of different ages, sex and class. Priestly also employs the method of a time shift, a favourite mechanism which occurs in some of his other plays, too. The plot is basically simple and although the central character is a police officer he is unlike any other policemen as rather than uncover the murderer he engages in a discussion about society.

Mr and Mrs Birling, who are very rich, he being a mill owner and expecting soon to be knighted, and their son Eric, are holding a party to celebrate the engagement of their daughter Sheila to Gerald who is heir to Mr Birling's business rival. Although the atmosphere is light-hearted there is a slight sinister undertow, and when the ladies 'withdraw' Mr Birling advises Gerald to look after his own and not concern himself with the community.

The doorbell rings and Inspector Goole enters and informs them that he has come to investigate the suicide of a young girl called Eva Smith that afternoon. When he sees a photo of the girl Birling admits that she was one of his employees whom he had sacked as she led a strike for more money, although he paid the usual rates. Sheila and Mrs Birling return and Goole tells them that Eva's next job was at a major department store. Sheila admits to having seen Eva smirking at her and threatens the manager that he would lose the Birling's very substantial account unless Eva were sacked. She now feels responsible for Eva's death. Eva, jobless, then changed her name to Daisy Renton and Gerald reveals that he knew her too. He met her at a variety theatre and she became his mistress until he severed the arrangement.

Gerald, shocked by what is being revealed, goes for a walk and it is Mrs Birling's turn to see the photo. She admits that she had seen the girl, who was pregnant, two weeks earlier when she had come to ask for money from a charity of which Mrs Birling was the chairlady; she persuaded the committee to refuse the request and is unwilling to take any blame for the girl's death. She denounces the child's father, but the father turns out to be Eric, her son. He, too, had met her at a theatre bar and they had had a sexual relationship; she had accepted money from Eric until she realised it had been stolen by Eric from his father's office.

It is clear, even to the Birlings, that they had each played a part in Eva's death; Sheila and Eric are contrite but their parents are concerned only with covering up their involvement. The inspector then delivers a 'no man is an island' speech in which he tells the Birlings that they were each responsible and that there are millions of Evas and 'John Smiths' out there all inter-twined with our lives and that if 'we' ignore our responsibility there will be blood and anguish; this was Priestley's message to the world and he lived long enough to see it being played out.

After the inspector had left Gerald returned; he had made enquiries and found out that there was no Inspector Goole in the force. They believe that Goole had tricked them and possibly shown them each a different photo. They phone the hospital which confirms that there has not been a suicide for months. The parents are delighted but Sheila and Eric maintained that nothing had changed as they had each committed the acts as accused. But there is general relief.

Yet the play is not yet over; the phone rings and is answered by Mr Birling. In a *coup de theatre* he informs the family that a young girl has committed suicide and that an inspector is on his way to ask questions. Final curtain.

Both *The Mousetrap* and *An Inspector Calls* have a twist at the end and each has a bogus policeman at its centre; but whereas Christie's play is an entertainment, *An Inspector Calls* is a vehicle for Priestley's warning to society. In each case, however, there is one policeman (or 'policeman') working alone who appears to be unconnected to any police force. And for all the complex plotting each playwright uses the format of the lone plain clothes detective first seen in *The Murders in the Rue Morgue*.

Tom Stoppard's brilliantly intricate play, first seen in 1968, is not only a play within a play where each play is a different farce, it is more like a chess game where not only the players but the pieces themselves also able to move, plus a couple of bystanders who can also influence the game. It is a romp and a farce but above all a spoof on country house whodunits—a mousetrap with no mice.

The play opens with a bare stage and two theatre critics, Moon and Birdboot, Moon by virtue of the unavailability of his superior, Higgs. Birdboot is interested in one of the actresses who has yet to appear. Both critics are in the audience, in front. The 'play' they have come to review takes place in Lady Muldoon's country residence and opens with a body on an otherwise empty stage. Enter the char, who, indifferent to the corpse, turns on the radio to hear the police explain that there is an escaped madman in the vicinity of the manor. Simon, who is in love (as is Birdfoot!) with the lady of the house, Cynthia, enters. All this is being watched indifferently by the two critics. Inspector Hound arrives to look for the madman, and the body is finally noticed. Everyone leaves to help Hound, and Simon is left alone and whilst bending to look at the body is shot dead. Whilst all this is going on the two critics discuss how they will write up the play, Moon's jealousy of Higgs, and Birdboot's love for the actress. As they talk the phone on the stage rings, Moon goes up and answers it and says to Birdboot 'It's for you': it is Birdboot's wife. He steps up on to the stage and the outer and inner plays are now linked. The 'play' restarts and being on stage after taking the phone call, Birdboot is now in it, recognises the body as that of Higgs, who was indeed unavailable, is mistaken for Simon and meets his end. Moon goes on stage to see why Birdboot was killed and is confronted by Major Muldoon, Cynthia's brother-in-law who accuses Moon of being the madman and shoots him. Moon dies and the Major announces himself to be the real Inspector Hound and also Cynthia's husband who disappeared ten years earlier. But the dying Moon recognises him as the third string critic who will now be number one.

Stoppard's play sheds no light on how stage plays reflect the police but is a razor-sharp dig at formulaic country house murder mysteries with a sub-text concerned with the interplay between fact and fiction. What Priestly did with time Stoppard did with space: made it intermingle and overlap. But then Priestly was being deadly serious whereas Stoppard was being flippant ... perhaps.

Film and television

Both the cinema and the television screen, which in many ways is merely a smaller version of the large screen, are better able than the stage to depict both action stories involving the police and crime mysteries in which the investigator is a police officer, either working on his own or with other officers. The difference between the two forms is that whereas the cinema showed full length films the stories on television were either in the form of short one act plays or a full length mystery broken into, usually, half hour or one hour episodes a number of which formed a series. Whereas a film is set in its time, a TV series which sometimes stretches over a number of years, can reflect changes in society, can comment on current issues and more directly reflect changing attitudes of society to the police.

In 1949 a full length film, *The Blue Lamp,* appeared showing a benign, caring, community-minded cockney copper called Dixon, played by Jack Warner. Warner, in real life, appeared to have many of the attributes of Dixon and was much admired by the public. In the film the police are depicted as friendly, communal and moral so it comes as a great shock when in the middle of the film Dixon is threatened by a gunman robbing a cinema, and when told to get out of the way he does not budge and is shot dead. It was almost as if Jack Warner himself had been shot and the film ends with a group of criminals getting together to hunt down Dixon's killer.

The first police series to be shown on television in Britain was the BBC's

Fabian of Scotland Yard which was broadcast from 1954 to 1956 and based on cases from real life. Other series followed but it was the TV spin-off from *The Blue Lamp*, *Dixon of Dock Green*, that became something of a legend and ran from 1955 to 1976. Its creator was Ted Willis and because of his considerable research the programme reflected the police of the time as recognised by the public — calm, orderly and friendly with Jack Warner brought back from the dead in the role of George Dixon.

Possibly buoyed by the success of *Dixon* the BBC launched a second police drama, *Z Cars*, in 1962, a series that ran for sixteen years. It is probable that *Z Cars* should have the accolade for bringing reality to British screens as it reflected the changing public perception of the police. Gone was the avuncular George Dixon and the quiet suburban streets which he patrolled. Instead there were police officers who were rough, tough, aggressive and sometimes violent, who operated in the grim and grimy streets of North West England. For the first time many viewers could see on their screens what they could see outside their front doors. Of course, during the span of years for which the programme ran, it, too, became formulaic but at least it was closer to the real world in Britain. The romanticised version of the police on the screens was giving way to the realistic view of the police seen by the public.

In 1919 twelve detectives were summoned to Scotland Yard and the 'Mobile Patrol Experiment' was founded. Later called the 'Flying Squad', they were authorised to operate anywhere in the Metropolitan Police District without observing divisions.

By 1970 the police were widely viewed as being ineffectual; a few years earlier three police officers were shot dead and the philosophy of policing that had lasted for more than a hundred years was seen as no longer relevant. Fast cars, chases and guns were regarded as more appropriate and this is what the government and television gave them.

ITV's answer to *Z Cars* was *The Sweeney* which ran for three years from 1975. 'Sweeney' is short for 'Sweeney Todd' which is cockney rhyming slang for Flying Squad. With John Thaw and Dennis Waterman as the detective inspector and his sergeant the series achieved great popularity, so much so that two cinema films. *Sweeney!* and *Sweeney 2* were produced.

On TV there were fifty-three episodes each running for fifty minutes and unlike previous 'cop shows' like *Dixon* which depicted a sanitised version of the police, *The Sweeney*, although rough and tough, had higher standards than the real Flying Squad which was involved in corruption and bribery and saw its real-life commander, Detective Chief Superintendent Kenneth Drury jailed for eight years after being convicted of five counts of corruption in July 1977, after which a further twelve officers were also convicted of corruption. Thus despite being criticised for its bad language, violence and corruption of police officers, *The Sweeney* still did not match the unlawful behaviour of the real thing. Since then The Squad (as it is still called) has foiled a number of robberies and arrested the robbers involved, including the Barclay's Bank robbery at Blackfriars, Southeast London; and in an operation involving 200 officers, the attempt in November 2000 to rob the Millennium Dome of the 200 carat Millennium Star valued at £200 million. In September 2007 it foiled a raid and shot dead two suspected armed men attempting to rob a G4S security van.

If the work of the uniformed police was fairly accurately depicted on screen and reasonably reflected the nature of policing as it changed during the 1960s, 70s and 80s, programmes about the detective arm of the police were highly glamorised.

The Bill, on ITV, was the longest running television series showing police procedures. The title is a variation of 'The Old Bill', slang for the police. The centre of the programme was the fictional police station of Sun Hill and each episode covered a single shift. Whereas *The Sweeney* depicted with considerable accuracy the work of the Flying Squad and the type of policing involving car chases and the interception of crime, *The Bill* depicted the work of the uniformed police operating from an ordinary police station, although it depicted violence from time to time.

The erosion of respect for the police that began in the late-1960s continued and there was a return to the screen of the sleuth. However, unlike the detectives in novels those on television were police officers resembling Adam Galbraith rather than Sherlock Holmes or Campion. Among these was *Taggart*, a police drama series set in Glasgow involving a senior detective with two or three assistants, one of whom, unusually, is a woman. *A Touch of Frost* first appeared in 1992. It featured the detective Jack Frost played by David Jason, a cantankerous and tetchy detective inspector who usually worked alone and, with no home life having been widowed during the series, appeared to work non-stop.

In 1990 a series was launched called *The Chief* which revolved around a new chief constable (played by John Stafford) of Eastland Police. He ruffled feathers early by appointing a female deputy and by being a tough, no-nonsense and politically liberal officer who was more involved with policy making than with management. He clashed with the Home Office and struggled against opposition from his own front line officers whilst his deputy had to fight against institutional sexism. *The Chief* ran until 1995 and was followed two years later by a detective series that could not be more different and which abandoned all pretence of reality.

The year 1997 saw the first episodes of a series that is still going almost twenty years later. *Midsomer Murders* starred John Nettles as DCI Tom Barnaby who in the course of many episodes has had as assistant a number of detective sergeants. Midsomer is a small village (several villages were used for the screenings) in a beautiful part of the south of England, but the combined murder rate over the series would make the death toll of a major catastrophe seem a minor mishap. There are usually a minimum of three murders per episode and although the plots are of a complexity unknown to Scotland Yard, Barnaby always gets his man, and sometimes woman. He is, of course, attached to a police force—he works for Causton CID—but he seems more semi-detached. He lives in the village with his wife who is often of more use than his sergeant, joins in village life and solves a multiple murder a week. In 2011 John Nettles left the show and his place was taken by Neil Dudgeon as DCI John Barnaby, Tom's younger cousin.

In the first episode an elderly woman was found dead at home and Barnaby suspected that she was murdered. There were many suspects and two further murders occurred in the course of the next two hours. A Canadian reviewer after seeing 'The Killing at Badger's Drift', called it '… another masterpiece [from Britain] maintains the standard which we are accustomed to' showing scant regard for the English language. If he regards *Midsomer Murders* as a masterpiece one wonders what he thinks of *Hamlet*. Ten years later, in 'The Animal Within', Faith Alexander, believing herself to be the inheritrix of her uncle Rex's will arrives at Midsomer and shortly after, Rex is fished out of the river, dead. It transpires that several other local residents have wills, there are two further murders and of course Barnaby solves them all.

In 2008 'The Sicilian Defence' was screened; it is not about chess strategy—it is much more complicated than that. Young Harriet, on her way to elope with Finn, is attacked in woods and it is a year later before she awakes just as the annual chess tournament is about to begin. The chess club's president is murdered; Harriet's father is murdered, too. Barnaby and Harriet's doctor take her to the woods where she had been attacked and her recalled memories lead to the killer—with the aid of Barnaby.

Setting aside the intricate plots, *Midsomer Murders* is about as simplistic as it is possible to achieve. Set in beautiful surroundings, episode after episode produce multiple murders solved by a detective notionally attached to a police force but working virtually alone. Tom (and later John) Barnaby, jolly, married, part of the community and amiable is the exact opposite of Adam Galbraith the lonely, unmarried introvert, but they could easily swap roles.

In some ways similar to *Midsomer Murders* was *Heartbeat* which was broadcast between 1992 and 2010. It took place in North Yorkshire and centred round a young couple: PC Nick Rowan and his new wife Kate, a doctor, both having moved to the small town of Ashfordly in Yorkshire. Unlike the DCIs that dominate other police dramas the main character is the village bobby, a mere PC. Although he is the central character other characters have major roles too. The programme reflected the times and occasional references to hippies, drugs and pop music gave a contemporary feeling. In many ways a far more realistic representation of the police and the time in which it was set, its cosiness is distant from the more realistic police dramas of the same era.

Death in Paradise is a sort of tropical *Midsomer Murders* with a lower body count. It was launched in October 2011 and is still running. It is set in the fictional island of Sainte-Marie and actually filmed in Guadaloupe in the Caribbean. Latterly the victims have been police inspectors sent from England to help run the island's crime detection service. In a recent episode DI Poole has been found on a veranda with an ice axe through his heart (who on a tropical island would own an ice axe?) and a replacement, DI Humphrey Goodman, played by Kris Marshall, arrives to investigate the murder. He is portrayed as a disorganized ditherer rather like the American detective Colombo, who takes notes of interviews on the back of his boarding pass and other bits of scrap paper; but he obviously has a fine mind that focuses on opportunity, means and motive, rather like Poirot. There are few contenders for the murder as he or she must be one of the Brits who knew DI Poole, and virtually no clues, but by a purely deductive process which eliminates suspects one by one and gradually focuses on the killer, he identifies not just the killer but the motive, which was to cover up a crime the killer committed some 25 years earlier.

Although the setting is a tropical Midsomer—a beautiful island compared with beautiful English countryside—the mechanism is pure Edgar Allan Poe. Like C Auguste Dupin, Goodman is faced with a murder seemingly with neither clues nor suspects and solves the problem by means of ratiocination. Not only that, but the format, like many other tales in all the media, is that of a single policeman working alone with (in this case) the island's few policemen acting as his aides plus one lovely lady police officer as his handmaiden and romantic interest.

The most popular detective mystery programmes from the 1980s until the end of the century was undoubtedly *Morse*, the title taken from the name of the principle character played by John Thaw, assisted by Detective Sergeant Lewis, played by Kevin Whately who work for Thames Valley Police. There were a total of thirty three episodes, some based directly on books by Colin Dexter and others written *de novo* by several other writers, but not Dexter who, however, appears fleetingly in every episode.

Morse tends to be irascible and morose; he is partial to opera, particularly Wagner, cryptic crossword puzzles, good beer and the Oxfordshire countryside. He is intelligent but very much a loner and although he has the occasional relationship with a woman they all come to nothing. Lewis, on the other hand, is a family man, fairly down to earth, not as incisive as Morse but is no fool. Although Morse is quite rude to him at times there is an obvious bond between them and, of course, all their cases are solved, sometimes by Lewis. It goes without saying that very little in these programmes remotely resembles how real detectives work.

The Morse series was hugely entertaining with the large helpings of the Oxfordshire countryside and the courtyards of the various Oxford colleges very pretty to look at. It is possible that not since Jack Warner playing Dixon has the public felt so warmly towards an actor as to Thaw playing Morse.

The end of the Morse series in 2000 coincided with the death of John

Thaw. In 2007 a spin-off series called *Lewis* was launched in which Lewis has been promoted to detective inspector still played by Kevin Whately, and he is assisted by James Hathaway played by Laurence Fox. They are no longer in the Thames Valley Police as that name is no longer permitted but are in the fictitious Oxfordshire Police Force. Lewis' personal situation has changed as his wife has been killed by a hit-and-run driver and he has become very friendly with Laura Hobson, the forensic pathologist; and he is intellectually outstripped by his assistant, the Cambridge educated and erudite Sergeant Hathaway. The plots of *Lewis* are very complicated but the episodes all have a similar structure: there is a murder in each half and much of the time Lewis and Hathaway walk around Oxford telling each other — and presumably the puzzled audience — what has been happening.

Colin Dexter's golden goose laid another egg in the form of a prequel to *Morse* called *Endeavour*, which was Morse's first name, and is about the younger Morse as a detective constable. In this series we are shown the development of Morse's intellect, his love of opera and his tendency to be right when everyone else is wrong. The first series was launched in 2013 but begins in 1965 when Morse joins the Oxford City Police CID. He impresses his superiors by solving a string of murders but is shot and injured and placed on light duties. In the second series it is a year later and young Morse returns to duty and continues to solve cases, and the series ends when he and others investigate a corruption and paedophile ring and Morse is arrested for the murder of the chief constable and placed in custody.

Wandering briefly into the realms of forensic science (see *Part 4*), the first episode of the first series got into trouble within a few minutes. Endeavour Morse visits a doctor for information. He says, 'We found a bottle of digoxin, which is a derivative of digitalis, isn't it? Quite dangerous, I would have thought, Dr Prentice?' 'Yes, quite lethal,' the doctor replies. 'It's not called deadly nightshade for nothing.' It is, in fact, not called deadly nightshade at all: digitalis comes from *digitalis purpurea*, the foxglove, whereas deadly nightshade, from which atropine is derived, is a common name for *atropa purpurea*. In the same episode, set in 1965, it was suggested that death was by Drinamyl which contains amphetamine. Quick on the draw Morse says, 'Amphetamines? They're illegal, aren't they? As of last year.' In fact, amphetamines are still legal, though controlled, and Drinamyl (purple hearts) were never banned but were voluntarily withdrawn in 1978.

Although this episode was screened in April 2013, the above errors were the subject of an article by Andrew Haynes in the 18th August 2014 edition of the *Pharmaceutical Journal* of the Royal Pharmaceutical Society of Great Britain.

In all three manifestations of Colin Dexter's character—Morse, Lewis and Endeavour—we see the same structure: Morse and Lewis, Lewis and Hathaway, the young Endeavour Morse—working within a police force but working alone, almost like private detectives using the facilities of the police. Although television programmes about the uniformed police give a reasonable insight as to how the police work, whether tearing up and down in cars or working in a police station, and also reflect society's attitude towards the police (and the police's attitude towards society), programmes about detectives bear little resemblance to how real life police detectives operate.

In 2013 a new episodic whodunit was launched called *Broadchurch*, the name of the fictitious town in Dorset in which this murder mystery is set. The first series (there is to be a second) was of eight episodes each lasting about one hour and revolved around the murder of eleven year old Danny, the son of Beth and Mark Latimer. There is a large cast which is needed to cope with complicated intertwining plots that are revealed as woodlice are revealed when a log is lifted. Detective Inspector Alec Hardy, an experienced city detective is called in by the local superintendent much to the chagrin of Detective Sergeant Ellie Miller who had hoped to head the investigation.

As the increasingly complex plot unfolds it appears that everyone in the town is up to no good: drugs, unaccounted cash, illicit sex, affairs and two red herrings: Danny's father, Mark, is taken in for questioning as he cannot account for where he was on the night of Danny's death (he was having sex with the hotel owner); and it was revealed that some years earlier Jack the newsagent had been jailed for sexually assaulting a minor, but as this is revealed in episode four he could not possibly have 'done it' with four more episodes to go. However, in episode five he reveals that he had had an affair with a 15-year-old girl whom he later married. Having tied up that false trail he does the right thing and jumps off a cliff. In the last episode D S Miller's husband Joe confesses to killing Danny who had threatened to expose Joe's excessive attentions towards him. It was with great prescience that Miller was not chosen to lead the investigation.

Broadchurch is a mixture, which may account for its popularity. On the one hand it is a straightforward murder mystery in a small town—the type of crime that Miss Marple might have dealt with; on the other, although the two detectives work together (Holmes and Watson; Lewis and Morse; Poirot and Hastings) they are clearly part of a police force with characters being brought in for questioning and usually released; the DI being astonished when told to scale back resources; and the occasional involvement of the forensic team. But there are no car chases, brutality or very foul language. It is more like a warmed up *A Touch of Frost* in which neither detectives nor the uniformed police bear much relation to what really happens.

☙

It is clear that if one wants to learn how the police work there is little point in studying books, plays or television fiction. The books are often carefully plotted mystery (usually) murders which are solved by a single detective or quasi-detective, often assisted by a policeman of lower rank. The real police are either not, or only marginally, involved.

As mentioned earlier, the number of professional stage plays is relatively small and they generally follow the format of the books and short stories. This is not surprising as one cannot do on the stage what is possible on film and television.

The nearest one gets to a realistic representation of how the police operate is on the large and small screen. Without the constraints of the page or the stage, police stations, car chases and so on can be shown as in, for example, *The Sweeney* and *Z Cars,* as well as the more static detective mysteries such as *Morse* and *Poirot.* The other big advantage that television has in particular, is the ability to keep up with and reflect changes in attitude to the police and to depict changes in society generally.

Part 2

COURTS AND TRIALS

CHAPTER 4

Introduction to Courts and Trials

In the same way that many members of the public have only a vague idea of the function of the police and how they operate, many people do not understand the criminal justice system and the role of the various courts. There is also a rather folkloric attitude towards sentencing: that it can come only after a fair trial and that there are maximum sentences for each offence are disputed ('Why waste time with a trial? Just lock him up and throw away the key'). Of course this attitude is completely reversed when the speaker is prosecuted for driving at 120 mph on the motorway ('I was in complete control. It's just that the police haven't got enough to do'), or nicking a few things from the supermarket ('Of course I intended to pay. A few bottles slipped to the bottom of the trolley'). If an offence of a sexual nature by a man comes into the public domain, no matter how minor or how long ago it was committed ('I was only seven at the time' said the grandmother of sixty-eight, 'but I remember it like yesterday') — many of us cannot remember yesterday too clearly — a popular advocated punishment for men is surgical excision of their organs of reproduction notwithstanding that this is a penalty not to be found on the statute book.

Short of appeals to the higher courts — the High Court, Court of Appeal or Supreme Court — in a criminal case, there are two types of court in which criminal proceedings take place. These are the magistrates' courts and the Crown Court. There are also civil courts where disputes are settled, when no crime has been committed (or at least not involving the arrest, charging and conviction of the perpetrator: criminal offenders can sometimes be sued in the civil courts). Although the higher courts will be mentioned here this is only for context as they are are rarely if ever fictionalised.

Trials in magistrates' courts are settled by justices of the peace (JPs), commonly known as 'magistrates' or 'justices'. These courts have a long history going back to the fourteenth century or even earlier although, of course, they have been altered and modified over the years. JPs are ordinary members of the public, that is, they do not have to be lawyers although some are. Men and women may be invited or nominated to become justices or can put themselves forward. If they pass selection and take the judicial oath, after a short period of training they may sit in court, decide whether defendants are guilty or not and if they are convicted, pass sentence (I describe my own experiences of being appointed JP in the *Introduction*).

It should be emphasised that the play by the English playwright Arthur Wing Pinero called 'The Magistrate', which concerns a JP caught up in scandalous events, is a farce and is by no means a true reflection of how real, unpaid, magistrates behave.

There is a maximum sentence for every offence, and guideline sentences for each offence so that there is a similarity of sentence within and between magistrates' courts around the country (England and Wales: Scotland and Northern Ireland have different systems). In addition to the (unpaid) magistrates, some courts employ a district judge, a title considered more dignified than the former 'stipendiary magistrate'. The DJs are lawyers, sometimes ex-justices' clerks, and they sit singly in court with a court clerk for company and perform the same function as the JPs. JPs usually sit in threes, sometimes only two, one of whom is the chairperson who has a speaking role but whose opinion carries no more weight than those of the other magistrates. As the cliché has it, the chairperson is are first among equals. They are addressed a 'Your Worship' or 'Sir' or 'Madam'. The court clerk, or legal adviser as he or she has become known, is in overall charge and ensures that the proceedings are carried out according to the law. If the legal adviser is not present the court is not in session. Magistrates also run the youth court where they can hear cases in which the defendant is aged from ten to seventeen. This court can hear some cases that for adults would be serious enough to be heard only in the Crown Court. They also hear cases in the family proceedings court, including certain partner disputes, care and adoption cases.

In a criminal case after the charge is read out by the legal advisor the defendant is asked if he or she pleads guilty or not guilty. If he or she pleads guilty the brief facts of the case are read out by the prosecutor and if a defence lawyer is present he will be asked if he or she wishes to say anything in mitigation, after which the magistrates proceed to sentence. If they all agree an appropriate punishment the chairman will announce the sentence there and then; if the magistrates do not agree, or if the conviction is for more than one offence, or if the circumstances of the case are unusual, or if the offender has previous convictions, they will most likely retire and discuss the offence and arrive at an agreed sentence. If there are three magistrates there may be a two to one decision, even if the 'one' is the chairperson; his or her vote carries no more weight. If a difficulty arises because of a legal problem or lack of understanding the adviser will be asked to join the magistrates in private to explain (or sometimes this process occurs in open court), but the adviser plays no part in determining guilt or a sentence. He or she can, however for example, tell the magistrates that a conviction or sentence they have arrived at is unlawful, in which case they will have to think again; or that the sentence, while lawful, is either very high or unusually low for that particular offence. With driving with excess alcohol, the legal limit is 35 micrograms of alcohol in 100 millilitres of breath. Every offence has a higher and a lower end. An offence of driving with excess alcohol in the breath may be the result of 40 micrograms per 100 millilitres or 350 micrograms. They will each involve a prosecution for driving with excess alcohol but the sentences should reflect the degree of intoxication recorded. If, in the opinion of the legal adviser, the penalty does not reflect the seriousness or otherwise of the offence he will point this out to the bench in which case they *may* think again and modify their sentence or not. Once the sentence is agreed the chairman will announce it in the court in an even voice: 'For the offence of driving with more than the permitted level of alcohol in your breath you will be fined £250 and you will be disqualified from driving for one year.' If, however, the level of alcohol is very high, the chairman might begin by saying 'This is a very serious instance of this offence as your alcohol level was more than twice the permitted limit…' and then announce a more severe sentence, which could be a higher fine, or a longer period of disqualification or both. Nowadays most punishments follow sentencing guidelines.

If the defendant pleads not guilty the procedure is different and more protracted. There will be a prosecutor from the Crown Prosecution Service (CPS) to call evidence for the prosecution in the form of witnesses and permitted written statements. The defendant may either defend himself or herself or be represented by a solicitor or a barrister. The proceedings begin with the prosecutor outlining the facts of the case, and he then calls witnesses if there are any. After each witness has sworn to tell the truth he or she will be asked questions by the prosecutor designed to demonstrate the guilt of the defendant. He or she may then be questioned (cross-examined) by the defendant or, if represented, by his or her lawyer, to show that the witness is wrong, misguided or even lying. After all the prosecution witnesses have given their evidence it is now the turn of the defence and the defence lawyer will call the defendant to the witness box where he or she, too, will swear to tell the truth. If the defendant is not represented the legal adviser will question the defendant sufficiently to establish what his or her case is. Once the defendant has been questioned by his or her own lawyer the prosecutor cross-examines him or her. Any witness for the defence will then be questioned and cross examined. Finally, first the prosecutor will address the court to show why the defendant is guilty, followed by the defence lawyer to show that he or she is not. After each side has had its say the justices will normally retire to their private quarters to discuss matters: it would be very unusual, and rightly construed as discourteous, if they announced a verdict without it being seen that they have considered the matter fully after a trial. If the justices convict the accused the procedure is then the same as for a guilty plea and the court will sentence him or her. If the justices find that the defendant is not guilty they will return to court and with the defendant standing the chairman will announce, 'The court finds that you are not guilty of the offence charged and you are free to go.'

The sentencing powers of magistrates are limited to (normally and at the highest end): a maximum fine of £5,000, up to six months' imprisonment or both (although planned increases have been mooted). Penalty points and/ or disqualification from driving are sometimes mandatory and sometimes an option in relation to driving offences.

All trials, whether for challenging a parking ticket, not paying your bus fare up to rape, murder and cannibalism begin in the magistrates' courts and more than sixty per cent are completed there. There are basically three grades of offence: those that are too serious for magistrates to deal when they can only be tried and sentenced at the Crown Court known as 'on indictment', including for example allegations of murder, rape and 'large scale' fraud; 'either way cases' such as theft and some assaults sent there by magistrates as a matter of procedural choice; and summary offences that can normally only be dealt with from start to finish by magistrates. Either way offences are dealt with in the magistrates' court unless *either* the magistrates *or* the defendant wishes the trial to take place in the Crown Court before a jury.

Leaving aside the Supreme Court and the Court of Appeal, the High Court can hear civil cases 'from scratch' but it also hears certain appeals and applications from the decisions of subordinate courts. It is divided into the Queen's Bench, Chancery, and Family Divisions. If there is a legally-based appeal (known as a case stated) this is heard by a Divisional of the Queen's Bench. The High Court also hears applications for judicial review of decisions of lower courts (normally those of magistrates' courts but occasionally of the Crown Court). High Court judges are referred to as 'Mr or Mrs Justice Black' and judges of the Court of Appeal as Lord or Lady Justices. Judges of the Supreme Court are known as Supreme Court Justices and Crown Court judges (also known as Circuit judges) as His or Her Honour Judge Pink. Recorders are lawyers who act as part time circuit judges.

The Crown Court is a criminal court that hears more serious cases with a judge and jury, but it also handles appeals from the magistrates' courts. It replaced the Assize Courts and Quarter Sessions in 1971. The Old Bailey is London's most famous Crown Court; its official name is the Central Criminal Court. Crown Court cases can be tried before a Recorder, a Circuit or a High Court judge.

It is often in the historic Assize Courts which dealt with the most serious cases that many dramatisations of famous murder trials of the past are set by film-makers, with the added bonus of ceremony, costumes, the grandeur of many of the old courtrooms and the added frisson that the accused might well be facing the gallows if found guilty.

Although trials in the upper courts are run and controlled by judges it is the jury that decides whether the defendant is guilty or not. A jury consists of twelve people, usually but not necessarily of mixed sexes, drawn randomly from the population. Whereas the judge ensures that the trial is run according to the law and will control the barristers (also known as 'counsel') or sometimes nowadays solicitors if they stray outside the rules, it is the jury alone that tries the case according to the evidence heard in court from the witnesses and from nowhere and nobody else. They should not be swayed by what they may read in the papers or hear in the media. Although they announce their verdict at the end of the trial as 'Guilty' or ' Not Guilty' that is not really what they have decided; what they decide is whether the prosecution has proved its case beyond reasonable doubt, or not. There is never a situation where the defendant has to prove that he did *not* commit the offence (though he or she is responsible for raising certain defences such as an alibi or self-defence, if appropriate, for the prosecutor to counter). This was enshrined at the House of Lords appeal in *Woolmington* [1935] when Lord Chancellor Viscount Sankey declared 'Throughout the web of English criminal law one golden thread is always to be seen ... No matter what the charge or where the trial, the principle that the prosecution must prove the guilt of the prisoner is part of the common law of England and no attempt to whittle it down can be entertained.' It is convenient to note here that the Supreme Court took over appeals from the House of Lords in 2009. It is a title long used in the USA and elsewhere.

Two other courts are included here not because they are not understood by a large section of the public but because a majority of the public *mis*understand them. They are not really part of the British courts system but they can have an influence in certain specific circumstances.

The European Court of Justice (ECJ) is not an appeal court over and above the Supreme Court in England. If an appellant is not satisfied with the outcome of an appeal to the Supreme Court (or possibly other courts) the ECJ is not the next stop; there is no next stop. The ECJ is a supreme court only for the *interpretation* of EU law. It has no other function.

Nor is it possible to appeal any decision of any court in England and Wales to the European Court of Human Rights (ECtHR). Appeals cannot be 'taken to Europe' as is often, wrongly, stated. What the ECtHR does is hear complaints concerning the European Convention of Human Rights and Fundamental Freedom. A litigant may complain to the ECtHR that English law has violated his or her rights. The European court cannot change the law of an EU member country but if there is a finding in favour of the litigant it is up to the UK government to decide whether to take any action and it must consider this. Courts in England and Wales are not bound to follow the decision of the ECtHR but should take it into account; However, they must act in accordance with the Convention Rights as they appear in the Human Rights Act 1998. Also, direct claims may be made under the Human

Rights Act 1998 against a public body for breach of Convention rights but this does not involve either of the European courts.

CHAPTER 5

Trials in Literature

Novels and short stories about criminal courts, lawyers and trials are not as prolific as those about crime and detection but the subject attracts a good many writers and a substantial following of readers. Criminal trials occur when somebody is accused by the police of committing a crime and it is denied by a plea of not guilty. Although most cases are heard in magistrates' courts before justices of the peace, most of the literature about trials concerns trials in Crown Courts (or old Assizes Courts: see *Chapter 4*) before a judge and jury. The reason for this is simple: Crown Court cases are usually concerned with more interesting serious offences such as murder, manslaughter, robbery, rape and fraud. While one can write a book or story about those subjects, what author is going to sit before his computer or notepad and write a tale about a morning at Willesden Magistrates' Court devoted to fare evasions on London buses or how Uxbridge magistrates dealt with an outbreak of shoplifting at Heathrow Airport? Moreover, nobody would want to read about such trivia any more than they would buy books about people going around doing good. Such subjects somehow lack the attention-grabbing interest that is generated when a Tory MP is found in a brothel wearing ladies' underwear, or a teacher roaming around Europe with a missing schoolgirl. Murder cases are still the most popular, both real ones in the newspapers as well as in fiction, although some of the *frisson* of excitement and horror disappeared with the abolition of the death penalty. 'You will go to prison for a minimum of twenty (thirty or even forty years by today's sentencing levels) cannot match the chilling horror of 'You will be hanged by the neck until you be dead', a sentence enhanced by the wearing of a black cap and for murderers with a literary bent by the penalty being announced in the future subjunctive.

It is not surprising that crime and court proceedings have attracted the attention of authors, since a trial has a beginning, a middle and an end, an ideal format for a story and in-built conflict, especially under the adversarial system where lawyers effectively do 'battle' to win the case for their client. Increasingly for example, so I am told, commissioners of TV programmes demand that they must contain 'jeopardy', uncertainty, peril and so on, something that can be observed every day of the week in programmes as diverse as dramas, reality TV shows and fly-on-the wall productions. There are always elements of jeopardy in a real life trial.

Sometimes the reader knows the full facts of the case and whether the defendant is guilty or not. An example of this occurs in *To Kill a Mockingbird* by Harper Lee in which a black man is charged with the murder of a white man in America's Deep South. The reader knows he is innocent, but does not know that the defence case handled by the book's hero, a small town lawyer called Atticus Finch, though skilfully conducted and beautifully written, will fail under the onslaught of racial prejudice. But most of the time the reader does not know all the facts and the outcome of this fictitious trial is not revealed until the end. But Ms Lee was not writing a page turner but a serious book about justice and injustice. The entire black population of the town is sitting in one section of the public gallery with Atticus' eight year old daughter. At the end of the trial, after the defendant has been found guilty by the all white jury and sentenced to death, as Atticus slowly walks to the exit of the court the entire watching black community rise to their feet to honour in the only way they could the lawyer who tried so hard but failed to save their man. In the most moving sentence of the book, the lady by her side says to the little white girl, 'Stand up, your father is passing'. In this short sentence Ms Lee, who is herself white, starkly contrasts the compassion of the black people against the inhumanity of the whites. This is no mere storytelling; this is literature.

Agatha Christie is well known for her detective fiction, often featuring Poirot or Miss Marple who always catch the criminal. But her short story 'Witness for the Prosecution', first published in 1925 in *Flynn's Weekly* with the title 'Traitor Hands', became very famous on account of a double twist at the end. Leonard Vole becomes friends with a rich elderly lady named Emily French. She is found murdered and Vole is the prime suspect, and when it is known that he is her sole beneficiary he is arrested for her murder. The evidence against him mounts up at his trial; then, surprisingly, his wife Romaine gives evidence not on his behalf but as a witness for the prosecution.

She said that on the night of the murder her husband had gone out and taken a crowbar with him and returned after ten with bloodstained cuffs which he burned. He threatened her into silence. The feeling of the court swings against him.

Then the counsel for the defence cross-examined her and accused her of having made the whole thing up. She was in love with another man, he said, and she wanted to send Vole to the gallows. Romaine audaciously denied this. Counsel then produced a letter which began, 'Max, beloved' and claimed that fate had delivered Vole into their hands. 'At last I shall have my revenge' she claimed, and explained that in court she would say that he had come home with blood on him and ends the letter, 'Happiness at last!' Confronted with this letter Romaine broke down and admitted she had lied and that Vole had returned home as he had said a little after nine. The prosecution was sunk and Vole was found not guilty.

Vole's Counsel suddenly realised that Romaine was an actress he had seen before, but it was some time until he met her again and she admitted she had made up her face and put on an act. When asked why she had put on such an elaborate act she replied that she had to save him, but realised that the evidence of a devoted wife would not be enough. Once the evidence of the letter had shown her evidence to be a pack of lies the sympathy would move to her husband. Max did not exist. She dared not risk giving conventional evidence. 'You see', she said to the lawyer, 'you *thought* he was innocent –' 'And you *knew* it? I see,' said the lawyer. To which Romaine replies in the last line of the story, ' … you do not see at all. I knew — he was *guilty!*'

Christie later did not like an ending where a murderer goes free and rewrote it in which Leonard has a mistress and is about to go away with her when his wife Romaine stabs him to death. Although the plot and the ending are ingenious it is all too contrived to be realistic and the actual trial occupies only a very short part of the story. Unrealistic or not, the short story was rewritten as a play and in 1957 was made into a film starring Marlene Dietrich and Charles Laughton.

Some early courtroom tales seem to pay scant attention to verisimilitude regarding trial proceedings. An example of this occurs in an early 20th-century story published in 1919 by J S Fletcher called *The Judge Corroborates* in which not only is the conduct of trials misrepresented but the entire plot depends on the misrepresentation. It also depended on what is called 'fingerprint theory and system' not being universally believed. The story concerns a professional burglar called Jack Gamble who is arrested by a police officer called Dickenson for burgling a house in north London. Gamble is well known to Dickenson and his fingerprints were found on a whiskey decanter and a glass; Dickenson is a great believer in fingerprints and often chants to himself the mantra *no two fingerprints are alike*. At his Old Bailey trial Gamble refused to be represented and sat quietly while two fingerprint experts conferred. They decided that the prints on the glassware were the same as were taken at the police station and elsewhere. There was other evidence to show that Gamble was away from his lodgings when the burglary was committed. That ended the seemingly overwhelming prosecution case and Gamble was then granted permission to give evidence on his own behalf. He gave alibi evidence to the effect that when the burglary was being carried out he was in Wimbledon, many miles away. He admitted that he was there for an unlawful purpose, namely to burgle the home of the judge trying his case. An associate of Gamble's suggested that they burgle in the same night the judge's home as it contained among other things many silver and gold trophies awarded to the judge when he was a young athlete, and a house in north-London, each carrying out one of the burglaries; but the burglary of the judge's house never happened.

Gamble chose the judge's house and said that he wanted to look it over from the outside first before attempting the burglary. He went to Wimbledon while his associate committed the burglary north-London. What happened next is that bit by bit Gamble describes the judge's house seen through a large picture window that looks out on the common. He not only describes the details of the room and its contents but also when the judge and his friend enter the room, and what they were wearing, and their movements. He asks the jury how could he have done the job in north-London when he was obviously in Wimbledon, and invites the judge to corroborate what he has just said. The judge replies that he is in a curious situation in being asked to be a witness as well as a judge. Had the case been tried by another judge he supposed that the prisoner would have raised the same defence and called him as a witness. He then proceeded not only to corroborate Gamble's evidence but to flesh out the details. He also pointed out that there are no trains between Wimbledon and King's Cross during the night so there was no means whereby Gamble could have got back to London to commit the crime for which he was being tried which took place between two and four in the morning. After being cross-examined and asked what proof he had that he had ever been in Wimbledon, Gamble triumphantly produced a ticket from Wimbledon to King's Cross with the correct date. The judge, who was no friend of the 'fingerprint system' addressed the jury on that subject and after twenty minutes the jury returned a verdict of not guilty.

Although the story was published in 1919 the year in which it is set is not shown. The station of King's Cross and St Pancras in North London was opened in 1907 and the line ran to Clapham Common. It was not until 1926 that the line was extended through Clapham South to South Wimbledon and a little beyond. This is the route that later became part of the Northern Line, an early section of London's 'tube'. So not only was it not possible to travel between King's Cross and Wimbledon at night, until 1926, seven years after the story was published, it was not possible to make this journey at all. Perhaps the author may be forgiven this lapse as he lived in Yorkshire.

After Gamble had departed for Australia to start a new life a colleague of his explained to Dickenson how the scam was done. They decided to burgle the north-London house and the judge's home on the same night; Gamble did the north-London job and his colleague, after noting all the details that Gamble gave the court, decided that the job could not be done that night. He gave all the details he had seen at Wimbledon to Gamble who used them as his alibi.

Two things are interesting about this story. First, the widely held doubts about the value of fingerprints is essential to the plot, but it was not long before fingerprint evidence was universally accepted and used to convict or clear suspects early in the 20th-century. A novel by Mark Twain, *Pudd'nhead Wilson*, published in 1893 includes a courtroom drama that turns on fingerprint identification. And in Conan Doyle's 1903 novel *The Norwood Builder*, the study of a bloody fingerprint helps Sherlock Holmes expose the criminal and free his client. Second, the behaviour of the judge was probably unlikely when the story was written: it would be outrageous today. As soon as his house was mentioned by Gamble as the cornerstone of his alibi the judge should have stopped the case and put it over for a retrial with a different judge. The idea of the trial judge acting as a corroborating witness for the defence is risible.

This short story is covered in some length since if ever an example is required of a plot involving a court case that departs from reality one need look no further than *The Judge Corroborates.*

A deliberate attempt at poking fun at the Bar and the courts that is more of a farce than a spoof, is a novel entitled *Law & Peace*, by Tim Kevan and published as recently as 2011. It is a sequel to *Law and Disorder.* The author is a barrister and practised law for some ten years. There is a disclaimer to the effect that all the characters are fictitious (they certainly are) and any resemblance to real persons, living or dead, is coincidental. It would be, however, remarkable if the characters resembled any real people, but to make sure, the author has deliberately given his characters silly names — BabyBarista (the main character), SlipperySlope, Up Tights, JudgeFetish and FanciesHimself, to name but a few. The book is a send-up of barristers, chambers, courts and judges. It is intended to be funny but whether it is will depend upon the reader's taste. But it bears little resemblance to what actually goes on in courts of law.

John Mortimer QC was a practising defence lawyer who was also a prolific author known for his fictitious character Horace Rumpole who defended clients, usually at the Old Bailey. Writing in 2008 (reprinted in *The Independent* on July 10 2014) Sir John, as he then was, pointed out some of the similarities to and differences between courtroom fiction and the real thing. Barristers, he implied, had to be actors: they had to adopt many roles and simulate anger and sorrow. They could also use boredom as a weapon but this would be of no use in a novel or on the stage, nor would the general noise, coming and going, interruptions and general hubbub.

Rumpole and his wife Hilda ('She who must be obeyed') are amusing characters and Rumpole himself is portrayed as a somewhat dishevelled lawyer who fights for his client in court, uses every ruse in the book and some that are not to get them off, and then, at the end of the day, retires to Pommeroy's Wine Bar for a glass or two of claret. But beneath all this make-believe the court scenes are accurate, notwithstanding the liberties Rumpole takes as an advocate and his tussles with judges; and he often cleverly slips in social comment. In 'Rumpole and the Honourable Member', from the 1978 collection of short stories *Rumpole of the Bailey*, he is defending a Labour Minister accused of rape. Mortimer emphasises through Rumpole's cross-examination of the putative rape 'victim' the need to ask distasteful questions. Whilst questioning his client he asks the MP which schools his children attended. The Minister replied, 'Sarah's at the Convent and Edward's down for Westminster'. To which Rumpole replies, 'And the loyal voters are down for the Comprehensive.'

In 'Rumpole and the Fascist Beast', from the same collection, Rumpole is asked to defend a leading member of the 'Britain First' Party who has been selected to stand as a parliamentary candidate at the next general election. An ex-captain in the Royal Army Pay Corps, he is accused of a public order offence under the Race Relations Act by shouting racist slogans at a rally. He asks Rumpole to get him the maximum of two years' imprisonment, which is of course not in Rumpole's remit as the man has pleaded not guilty. At the same time a young Indian lawyer appears in Rumpole's chambers looking for a post. Rumpole takes him on as a junior in defiance of the colour prejudice of some of the other barristers. Rumpole, in his closing speech points out to the jury that his client is living in the past age of the Empire and the Raj. He tells them that he flies a Union Jack from a flagpole outside his house and lowers it at sunset. He ridicules him to the point where the jury first smile and then laugh; they do not take him seriously as a political threat and after only thirty minutes find him not guilty. The defendant is furious. At a special meeting of the Britain First Party the committee consider that he has not lived up to the Party's beliefs and he is stripped of his parliamentary candidature. Meanwhile the Indian lawyer is voted into chambers but decides he wants to prosecute so declines the offer. The discredited fascist shoots himself for the ridicule he brought to his Party and to himself; he would have preferred a long prison sentence to demonstrate his credentials as a Britain First supporter. Being acquitted brought him only shame.

Rumpole's client is clearly guilty under the Act but Rumpole's job is to get him off even though he finds his beliefs repugnant; Mortimer shows clearly in this short tale just how effective ridicule can be in a court trial.

The Return of Rumpole (from a brief retirement in Florida) is a novella that shows the seamier side of barristers' chambers. His chambers have replaced him with two new barristers so that on his unexpected return he finds that not only have two people moved into his room, but there is no room for him as the chambers are crowded to the limit. A good deal of nastiness creeps in when one of the new boys contrives to get him pushed out. Meanwhile Rumpole is involved as leading counsel for the defence in a murder trial, which he wins, during which the trial judge, a bête noire of Rumpole, makes the most outrageous interruptions and shows his support for the prosecution case. No doubt there are some chambers where the occupiers behave as Mortimer's characters do; but no Old Bailey judge would behave like Mr Justice Bullingham does.

A contemporary of John Mortimer was another barrister, indeed, a judge, Henry Cecil. Cecil was also a prolific writer but his novels did not contain many laughs as did the works of Mortimer who sent up many of his characters; what they did do was to illustrate the workings of the courts through fiction that was often witty. An example of this is his novel published in 1954 called *According to the Evidence*.

A girl is found murdered on the local common and a man, Gilbert Essex, has been charged with her murder. The opening chapter is largely a realistic verbatim account of prosecution and defence counsel's opening remarks followed by the examination and cross-examination of the defendant and the one witness, who was on the common at the same time. The chapter closes with the jury retiring to deliver their verdict. In the jury room the jury are undecided.

In the next chapter there is a party in the home of the defence counsel, Duffield; he arrives and announces that his client was found to be not guilty but nobody is pleased, not even Duffield, as they all believed him to be guilty. It is then revealed to the reader that the defendant was indeed guilty; he had killed before and would probably kill again. In the course of the next two months he does kill girls again, twice more, but the police have no evidence against him. Then he is found dead. One of the guests, Alec Moreland, who had been at the defence counsel's party, an artist who had been a commando in the war, tells his new fiancée Jill that he had killed Essex — in fact executed him — to stop him from killing more girls. He had no sooner asked her to marry him when an inspector calls and routinely asks him questions about his movements. It transpires that the police had found near the scene of the crime the chewed end of a pencil of a make that Moreland sometimes uses.

Alec Moreland's fiancée Jill calls on Ambrose Low, a friend who between the ages of twenty and twenty five had engaged in a life of crime but was never caught and had later, as a private enquiry agent, managed to get his father-in-law, a judge, acquitted of a murder charge and then married his beautiful and talented daughter. Jill tells Low that her fiancé did not kill Essex but is worried that he might be charged. Low advises neither of them to go to the police and points out that the fiancé should say nothing to the police and let the matter drop; if he didn't do it he has nothing to worry about. After Jill has left, Low's wife returns and he tells her he has just seen the girl who was going to marry the man who killed Gilbert Essex. Then Low calls on Alec and offers to help. Alec resents his visit and insists he needs no help as he had nothing to do with the death of Essex. After discussing Low's visit with his fiancée he decides to call on Low and admits to him that he had been hasty and asks how he can help. Low listens to Alec's version of events — he had lost a pencil; he had been in the woods near the cliff — and told him he had nothing to fear. Then he visited the police inspector offering information; the inspector told him he did not need to be told how to do his job. Shortly after, the inspector is told by his superior officer to visit Low and eat humble pie. He does so and is advised to go to the Lion in Medlicott, where Essex lived and was killed, and look at the visitors' book. The landlord reluctantly lets him look and he sees the name Alec Moreland. After he leaves the landlord tears out the pages with Moreland's name and burns them.

The inspector then calls on Alec who declined to answer any questions. A superintendent calls on Jill and implies that Alec is a suspect. The police question Alec's fiancée and Alec is arrested for murder. Committal proceedings are described and as Alec and Jill are now married she exercises her right to refuse to give evidence against her husband.

Cecil now introduces a comic character into the plot, one Colonel Basil Brain, who is supplementing his army pension by doing a little gardening. Low calls on him and asks him to ingratiate himself with Alec as a gardener and to say, 'I'd like to shake by the hand the man who killed Gilbert Essex.' After much practice the colonel gets it right. On a subsequent visit Low persuades Brain that Alec replied, 'I'll give you the opportunity.' When Low was confident that Brain knew his lines he suggested to the inspector that he visit the colonel and ask him if he had had a conversation with Alec

Moreland about Essex.

The cross-examination of the colonel by Duffield in the magistrates' court is hilarious and a tribute to Henry Cecil's versatility as a writer in that every wacky response that Brain gave to the prosecutor's questions actually made sense yet was never the answer that Duffield hoped for.

To cut a not very long story short, after a higher court trial in which there is another hilarious scene with Colonel Brain in the witness box, the trial is stopped and Alec is discharged.

In this short novel Cecil manages to describe accurately proceedings in the magistrates' and the higher court; to show how the police operate and, importantly, to demonstrate how a court can arrive at the wrong decision for the right reasons: according to the evidence.

Many of the short stories of Henry Cecil are extremely short, sometimes just six or ten pages. They often feature judges in and out of court and share no cast of characters as do the stories of John Mortimer. Cecil's tales are not rumbustious as are those of Mortimer, are sometimes whimsical and often have a surprise ending. Many, but not all, have plots linked to court procedure, or the role of judges and juries.

In *I Killed Gordon McNaghten* the narrator states that he once knew a man who was charged with murder and who was sorry that the death penalty had been abolished in 1957; in fact it was not finally abolished for murder until twelve years later. Jimmy is acquitted of murder thanks to alibi evidence given by his friend the narrator who lied in court. Some time later Jimmy approached a newspaper with the information that he had been, in fact, guilty of murder and sold them a story. He said that the alibi was false and he was aware that he could not be tried for an offence of which he had been acquitted. The public and Parliament did not like the idea of a confessed murderer flaunting his crime and going free, so he was arrested again and he was charged with two alternative charges: perjury and obtaining money by false pretences. There follows arguments in court first from defence counsel, that he should not be tried on both counts together, and then by the prosecuting counsel that he should be. The judge decided in favour of the prosecution and Jimmy was tried on three counts of perjury and a single count of obtaining money under false pretences. The jury believed his newspaper story but not what he said in the witness box and he was convicted on three counts of perjury for which he received five years on each count which consecutively totalled fifteen years in prison. Before he was taken down he complained to his friend the narrator that he was worse off than if he had been convicted of murder and they had not abolished capital punishment. The story ends with Jimmy saying he was innocent and the narrator saying that he knew his friend was indeed innocent of murder and perjury, because *he* had killed Gordon McNaghten. Nowadays in relation to certain serious crimes such as murder, the much vaunted double jeopardy rule under which, in England and Wales, someone cannot be tried twice for the same offence, does not apply and old acquittals can often be tested in the DNA-age. It still applies to other crimes.

Many of Cecil's short stories deal with little known minutiae of the law, and of criminal procedure. An example of this is *The Lesson,* a beautifully written story so taut and concise that it almost defies condensing. It deals with a little known point of law which may never have actually arisen in practice. The prisoner William Pellet had just been acquitted by the jury and the judge accordingly discharged him but then went on, 'in my opinion you have been very lucky in your jury. I hope at any rate you will have learned your lesson from these proceedings.' Pellet went straight round to a firm of solicitors. He showed them the evening paper: 'Acquitted prisoner lucky in his jury' and asks if he can sue for slander by the judge. He is told that a judge or counsel cannot be sued for anything they say in court in the course of proceedings because it is a privileged situation. But, Pellet persisted, the jury had said not guilty and the judge had discharged him: the proceedings had concluded and his name had been smeared. The solicitor says he cannot see an action for slander succeeding: it would be struck out: no trial.

However, after taking counsel's advice the solicitor writes to the judge in the most elegant and delicate terms asking if he would be prepared to give a public apology and pay a sum in damages. To cut a short story shorter the Master, and the Court of Appeal, dismissed the appeal even though the latter court stated 'it could never be right for a judge to cast doubt upon the correctness of a verdict of not guilty'. Criminal appeals then usually came before the Court of Criminal Appeal (now the Court of Appeal (Criminal Division)) whose judges agreed that they could please themselves what they could say in their own court.

A few months after the trial, one night two masked men entered the judge's house where he lived alone. They stripped and tarred and feathered him. He was shortly found by the police and conveyed to hospital. The police called on Pellet who told them either to arrest him or go away. The police were dogged, however, and eventually charged him with assault occasioning actual bodily harm and he was committed by the magistrates to the Old Bailey. There was considerable evidence against him and the judge gave a 'guilty summing-up'. After three hours the jury returned a verdict of not guilty. The judge said: William Pellet, the jury have found you not guilty and you are discharged. In my opinion you are –'. He paused. 'Yes?' said Pellet enquiringly. 'Discharged', said the judge. 'Call the next case'.

A budding law student could learn a lot from this six page story.

જી

Some of the stories outlined above are so contrived as to bear little relationship to what actually goes on in court. Although Crown Courts are, as John Mortimer has written, places where there are many comings and goings, a hubbub of noise, and to someone new to the scene, seemingly chaotic goings on. But beneath this apparent chaos there is a strict structure that is invariably followed. Each character has a part to play: the prosecutor has to demonstrate beyond reasonable doubt using the available evidence that the defendant committed the offence of which he or she is accused. The defence counsel's job is to show that the prosecutor has failed to do that. Witnesses must tell the truth. The jury must arrive at a decision based only on what they have heard in court. And the judge is there to ensure that the correct procedure is followed; that counsel do not overstep the mark and ask witnesses questions that are not permissible, or harass them; nor try to influence the jury by irrelevant information or by an over-seductive or aggressive manner. The judge is also there to sum up the evidence at the end of the trial, to advise the jury of the law and answer any questions they might have. If the jury bring in a verdict of guilty it is the judge who decides the sentence and announces it in court. In real courts that is what happens.

In much of the fiction involving court trials the judge often behaves in a manner that is rarely, if ever, seen in reality. During a trial the judge may be sorely tempted to intervene with a 'clever Dick' remark, or comment on what has been said, or address the jury with a remark indicating his own view of a witness' answer. But they keep their mouths shut except when it is their turn to speak. Advice given to chairpeople of magistrates' courts is just as valid for judges: to have a strong bladder and a still tongue. Alas, that does not always make good fiction.

To be fair to the authors of stories and novels that hinge on criminal trials, they are not writing the *All England Law Reports*, they are writing fiction for entertainment. It is of course possible to write a crime story in which a trial follows correct procedure where jokes or funny remarks from the participants would not be out of place. But even where the characters are not amusing, some stories, such as *The Judge Corroborates* are so contrived as to be quite unrealistic. If it is a good story does it matter? Is *Crime and Punishment* realistic: how many people would behave like Rashkolnikov? Are the rough tales of Mark Twain, the saccharin novels of Jane Austin or the wonderful short stories of Margaret Attwood realistic? The test in these, and other, books is not that the events described never happen, they are great books because the events described *could* happen. In Henry Cecil's *The Lesson* the remark made by the judge on which the story depends may never ever have been uttered; but it could have. Would King Lear really be so stupid as to carve up his country and distribute it to his three daughters? Later in the play, when his madness becomes evident, it is clear that he was mad at the beginning and his actions made sense. Charles Dickens' long novel *Bleak House* is about a legal battle lasting many years leading to a trial that never takes place. Such a battle and such a trial in the real world has never happened. But what makes it a great book is that all the events *could* and *might* come to pass.

Although some writing about court trials, and crime fiction in general, is downright bad, much of it, though contrived, though not following the reality of court proceedings, can still be a good read and give enjoyment to thousands. Neither of the two barristers, Cecil and Mortimer, who knew the court procedure inside out, departed from the reality of the court trial process, but should an obsession with what is 'real' deprive us of the wit of Henry Cecil or the clever buffoonery of Horace Rumpole or the ridiculously contrived plots of many other writers?

CHAPTER 6

Trials in the Theatre

In 1995 it was the 80th birthday of the American playwright Arthur Miller who died ten years later, and in 2009 another playwright, Harold Pinter, died. They were two of the three greatest writers for the stage in the post-war era (Tennessee Williams being the third), Pinter being awarded the Nobel Prize for Literature and Miller deserving to be awarded it.

Although Miller was fifteen years older than Pinter and they lived three thousand miles apart, their backgrounds were remarkably similar. Miller was born in Harlem, New York City, in 1915 to Polish Jewish immigrants Isadore and Augusta. Isadore owned a women's clothing company which he lost in the depression when they had to move to a smaller house in Brooklyn. Arthur delivered bread every morning before school to add to the family income. Pinter was born in 1930 to parents, Hyman and Frances, who were born in England of Jewish East European (Polish and Russian) ancestry. Hyman was a ladies' tailor and Frances was a housewife. He lived in Clapton in north-east London and attended Hackney Downs ('Grocers') school where he excelled in English, cricket and running. One other twist of fate links these outstandingly gifted writers. Miller's first play *The Man Who Had All The Luck* was withdrawn after four days when it first appeared; Pinter's *The Birthday Party's* first outing lasted five.

But what relevance does the law have to plays in the theatre? The answer regarding these two writers is easy: they were both committed to justice. Justice is to be found not only in the courthouse, but from the Greeks onwards has been the subject of some of the world's greatest dramas. Three of Miller's plays deal with the subject directly. *All My Sons* concerns a man who had sold defective aero engines to the US air force; the play takes place many years later when events catch up with deadly consequences. One of the 20th-century's greatest plays, *Death of a Salesman,* is about social injustice and questioned the reality of the American Dream; and, of course, *The Crucible,* in which an actual trial takes place, equated the witch hunt by

Senator Joseph McCarthy (before whom Miller himself refused to co-operate) and the witch hunt in Salem, Massachusetts in the 17th-century. In the mid-1960s Miller became the president of PEN and fought against the censorship, persecution and imprisonment of writers.

Pinter was overtly political. He wrote about oppression, menace and the unreliability of memory, the latter a problem very germane to court trials. A character in *Old Times* says, 'There are some things one remembers even though they may never have happened. There are some things I remember which may never have happened but I recall them so they take place'. In an early play, *The Birthday Party*, when Stanley, who is a lodger in Petey's boarding house, is being carried away by two unknown men for an unknown reason to an unknown destination, Petey calls out, 'Don't let them tell you what to do, Stan'. This was Pinter's trademark, his call to arms: don't let other people tell you what to do. He never let people tell *him* what to do. In *The Birthday Party* the victim, Stanley, is English; his abductors are Goldberg and McCann. Is this an old 'Englishman, an Irishman and a Jew' veiled joke or is Pinter hinting that Jews and Irish people, traditionally victims, can be oppressors too. If that were not widely recognised in 1958 when the play first appeared, there can be little doubt of its truth today.

In 1985 Pinter and Miller were both vice-Presidents of PEN and visited Turkey as an expression of solidarity with writers there and to investigate allegations of torture. At that time Turkey was a military dictatorship endorsed by the USA. At the end of their visit they were invited to a dinner hosted by the USA ambassador in the embassy in Ankara in honour of Miller. After the meal Miller gave a short speech in which he pointed out that Turkey, to which the USA was a generous paymaster, was a catastrophe. He asked, if the USA is a democracy, why support military dictatorships around the world? In Turkey there were hundreds of people in prison for their thoughts, persecution subsidised by the USA. After thanking Miller for his speech the ambassador cornered Pinter and pointed out that with Russians over the border they had to bear in mind the diplomatic, political and military realities. Pinter replied, 'The reality I have been referring to is that of electric current on your genitals.' The ambassador pointed out that Pinter was a guest in his house and Pinter left. They were both banished. Pinter later said that being thrown out of the USA embassy in Ankara was one of the proudest moments of his life. The plight of the Turkish Kurds prompted the short — fewer than a thousand words — play *Mountain Language* which concerned a minority population which was banned from using its own language. When he received the Nobel Prize Pinter was too ill to attend the ceremony but sent a video of his acceptance speech which was a long indictment of USA foreign policy.

There are a number of other writers whose underlying theme is justice — it is easy to recall Dickens and Mrs Gaskell, Disraeli, the South American Gabriel García Márquez, the Americans Sinclair Lewis and Clifford Odetts, the Chinese Lao She and Lu Xun among many others. They did not bring justice to the world but showed how unjust the world is. They are like the candle in *The Merchant of Venice* (Act V sc.i):

> How far that little candle throws his beams!
> So shines a good deed in a naughty world.

చ∕౧

Harold Pinter pointed out that there is no hard distinction between the true and the false, or between the real and the unreal. What a character on the stage says is real; but it is also unreal because he is merely an actor reciting lines. What he says is also true; but it is also untrue for the same reason. This blurring of reality and truth is remarkably brought into sharp focus in Tom Stoppard's *The Real Inspector Hound* in which Birdfoot and Moon are both critics of a play they are watching and also actors within it. Are they real or unreal? Is what they say true or untrue? Does a verdict of guilty beyond reasonable doubt mean that the defendant's guilt is real? Does 'Not Guilty' but not 'innocent' (see the *Introduction*) mean anything in the world beyond that of the court?

Another of Stoppard's plays dabbles with this conundrum. *Rosenkrantz and Guildenstern are Dead* concerns the two characters in the title who have relatively minor roles in *Hamlet*. But when they exit in Shakespeare's play they come into existence in Stoppard's. After they have left a scene in *Hamlet* they are backstage (in a scene onstage) and discuss with each other and any other character who is not onstage what is going on in the play. They are not real to begin with—they are actors reciting lines—but are they any less real backstage because for the time being they are not in *Hamlet,* or more real because they are discussing the goings on in a play they will shortly rejoin? But if they discuss the play with their wives after the show instead of with each other, is that a different kind of reality? And is what they say to their wives more true than what they say to each other? Is what they say onstage less or more true than what they say offstage, when as far as the audience is concerned they are still onstage?

A witness in a trial consolidates an alibi defence by stating that the defendant spent the night with her at the time the crime was committed. After leaving court she tells a friend that what she said was not true and that she had not seen the defendant for weeks: she had lied in court. But in reality she did spend the night with the defendant but did not want her friend to know that she was in an illicit relationship with him. So she told the truth in court and lied to her friend. If nevertheless the defendant is found guilty the reality for the defendant is that the jury did not believe her evidence, or his. At this point reality and truth diverge. After the case both counsel meet in the robing room. The defence counsel says that he had to run the alibi defence as he had nothing else. The prosecutor says he found the woman a convincing witness. The end result is that the defence did not believe its own main witness; the prosecutor believed her and challenged her evidence because that is his function. The jury decided that the witness had lied although she had told the truth. The witness had told the truth but lied to her friend so that she would not believe the evidence she gave in court. The defendant is sent to prison for a crime he did not commit. Among this tangled web of lies and truth, real and unreal, the jury have to contend with 'reasonable doubt'.

A Crown Court is very much like a theatre. There is a stage where the main actors play their given roles: defendant, counsel, witnesses, judge and jury. A supporting cast is in attendance. The principle performers dress in colourful clothes (judges) and dark clothes and wigs (barristers). They subsume their real identity in their roles by referring to each other as 'my learned friend' and to the judge as 'Your Honour' or 'My Lord/Lady'. There is an audience in the public gallery. There is a plot and there is a beginning and an end. As in most plays there are three Acts: the prosecution case, the defence case, and the judge's summing-up followed by the jury's verdict. There is uncertainty right to the end, as in a play. What will the verdict be? If guilty, what is the sentence? Who exactly are all these witnesses? How many of the witnesses are lying or are their memories at fault?

The aim of each of the two counsel, prosecution and defence, is to convince the jury that their version of events is correct; the defence needs to show that at least there is reasonable doubt and that the prosecution has not proved its case; the prosecutor hammers home the facts that point to the defendant's guilt. But the jury does not come from Mars. It is drawn randomly from the population and when it comes into court the jurors do not enter an unknown wonderland: they have been steeped in television, radio and films for years. The barristers do not have to measure up to how the jurors might expect them to perform; they are measured against barristers they have watched or listened to for entertainment. It becomes incumbent, therefore, for the lawyers to put on a show, to become entertainers as well as advocates. However clever the argument, a poor performance will not receive many brownie points. If that is not enough, they must also be alert to help an inarticulate witness who is favourable to their case and to disrupt the articulacy of those witnesses who are not.

But there is one major difference between the Crown Court and the theatre. Unlike the actors who wipe off their greasepaint at the end of a show and tell each other, 'You were wonderful, darling,' the principle performers in court are elated or dismayed at having won or lost a case, or go home to celebrate, or are taken to prison. 'Justice' is considered to have been done. However, although the Crown Court and the theatre have many similarities, courtroom trials occur relatively infrequently on the stage. The reason for this is not the lack of dramatic impact but that trials are very static. Apart from different people entering and leaving the witness box who are examined and cross-examined by counsel, there is very little real activity and the play could easily become 'wordy'; and the random coming and going and constant hubbub would have to be omitted, adding to the static presentation. However, there are some plays that contain a court trial within them.

Events in which life and art were turned upside down, Jeffrey Archer's bizarre play *The Accused* was written and performed whilst he was awaiting trial and as it turned out imprisonment for perverting the course of justice

some ten years earlier. Archer is Britain's top earning storyteller whose books
have sold over 250,00 copies. He is a former Member of Parliament and
Deputy Chairman of the Conservative Party. He was created a Life Peer in the
Queen's Birthday Honours of 1992 as Baron Archer of Weston-super-Mare.
He has written ten novels, several of which have been serialised for television
and radio, four sets of short stories, and three plays. His first—the court-
room drama *Beyond Reasonable Doubt*—starring Frank Finlay and Wendy
Craig, ran at the Queen's Theatre, London for over 600 performances. The
London *Evening Standard* had this to say about his 2000 play *The Accused*:

> As every critic in the land has noted, Jeffrey Archer's courtroom drama, *The
> Accused*, is a dreadful play, dreadfully acted, and an astonishing act of sheer gall
> on the part of its writer and star.

> What no one has so far said is that it's also the most compelling drama currently
> being performed in the capital. It's like watching a three-hour car crash—appall-
> ing, horrific, but you can't tear your eyes away. Even Archer's harshest critics must
> concede that, for all its faults, *The Accused* is unmissable.

> [His] tale…is a hackneyed, plodding mass of cliché. If anyone else had written
> it, it would have been rejected by every management in London. If Archer were
> not also appearing in it, no one would go to see it. It is his presence and his
> performance—completely wooden apart from his brass neck—that makes the
> play so utterly riveting, and even rejuvenates the old-hat technique of casting
> the audience as the jury…[It] represents a fascinating nexus between our mania
> for celebrity, and the increasing popularity of "reality"TV shows. It suggests that
> Archer has his finger closer to the contemporary pulse than his writings would
> lead us to believe…in the theatre's first "reality" courtroom drama, we can watch
> Archer—peer, politician, hack novelist and huckster—pre-empt his forthcoming
> perjury trial, and hint teasingly at the past court cases that led to it. It's like watch-
> ing a turkey-cock displaying his tail-feathers while on the abattoir conveyor-belt.

The play *A Pin to See the Peepshow* is a regular in local rep and is based
on the killing, trial, conviction and execution of Edith Thompson. The title
plays on the fact that such morbid stories are unavoidably fascinating in the

same way that Penny Dreadfuls were. It is a mix of trial and punishment and formats: book, play, films (including under other names). It also features as a chapter in a book cataloguing plays about crime called *Blood on the Stage, 1950-1975: Milestone Plays of Crime, Mystery, and Detection* by Amnon Kabatchnik. Another striking feature is that the play itself was banned by the Lord Chamberlain under the then rules.

☙

Although Jewish merchants and moneylenders visited and did business in Venice as early as the 10th-Century it was not until the 13th-century that they began to settle there. Jews were being increasingly harassed in their native lands — Spain, Portugal and Eastern Europe — so gradually drifted to Venice where, if not welcomed with open arms, they were tolerated and left alone. In 1290 Jews were not allowed to reside in the main part of the city, although allowed to work there, but had to pay a tax of five per cent on all import/export transactions. They settled on one of the islands that make up Venice, that of Spinalonga. In 1385 Jewish moneylenders were allowed to work in Venice; they had to pay a special tax but were given land for a Jewish cemetery. Various enactments between the 12th and 16th-centuries identified Jews by making them wear items of a particular colour and restricted them in the employment they were allowed to pursue. In 1492 Spain and Portugal expelled all the Jews living there and many Spanish and Portuguese Jews found their way to the relatively liberal city-state on the north-east coast of what is now Italy.

Gradually the number and importance of Jews in Venice increased so that by 1516 the Republic of Venice enacted a decree to organize them so that they were obliged to live in one area of the city, the site of an old iron foundry ('geto', pronounced 'jetto' in Venetian), and wear a mark of identification. Neither Yiddish nor Hebrew have a soft 'g' so the Ashkenazi Jews from mid- and Eastern Europe transformed the pronunciation of 'geto' to 'ghetto' with a hard 'g'. The ghetto was closed at night. However, the 16th-century ghetto had none of the connotations of those of the 20th; the Jews were not imprisoned in them, they only had to reside there; they were there for their safety. Jews had to manage the city's pawn shops at a fixed rate, but they were also given protection and allowed to practise Judaism. However, they were permitted to work only in pawn shops, as moneylenders, in the Hebrew printing presses, to trade in textiles and to practise medicine. In an increasingly anti-Semitic Europe, Venice was a relatively safe haven for Jews.

This is the environment in which we find Shylock.

Shakespeare's play *The Merchant of Venice* takes place some time in the 16th-century and is probably the earliest play to have a trial scene. The play was written by an Englishman but it takes place five hundred years ago in a foreign country; yet there are still aspects of the trial that are relevant in English courts today.

The play begins with Antonio, a rich trader, bemoaning to his friend Bassanio that one of his three ships out on the high seas has failed to return. Notwithstanding the blatantly anti-Semitic attitude displayed in the presence and in the absence of Shylock, a Jewish merchant and moneylender, when Antonio's second ship fails to return and he is desperately short of money he turns to Shylock for a loan until his third ship returns. Shylock does not particularly like Antonio or his views but knows him to be an honest merchant and immediately lends him the three thousand ducats requested with repayment by a stated date. When Antonio asks what forfeit he wants, that is if he fails to repay by the agreed date what would he take instead, Shylock, confident of repayment in time, jokingly suggests he will have one pound of Antonio's flesh to be taken from near his heart. Antonio and Bassanio join in the laughter at such a jolly jest and they all leave happy, Antonio with three thousand ducats that will save his business.

Whilst various sub-plots are being played out, including the problems caused by Shylock's daughter Jessica being in love with a Christian, Antonio's third ship fails to return and he is unable to honour his debt. Shylock goes to court to claim his pound of flesh and what began as a joke rapidly turns into a nightmare. The court case that follows in Act IV Scene 1 becomes the hinge on which the whole play swings.

The Duke of Venice presides and although he is more like a referee than a judge he begins by greeting Antonio and expressing his pity for him. Shylock he calls an inhuman monster. Antonio concedes that the duke has done all he can and he is prepared to submit himself to Shylock's rage. The duke opens the trial and says that Shylock merely means to frighten Antonio not to inflict the penalty on him. Shylock digs in his heels and knowing that tiny Venice thrived largely because its laws were universally accepted, points out that if he is denied these very laws will carry no weight:

> 'If you deny me, fie upon your law!
> There is no force in the decrees of Venice.'

Antonio's friend Bassanio offers Shylock six thousand ducats, twice the sum owed. Of course, he could have given Antonio three thousand of them before they walked into court, but that would have ruined the play ('Here's the three grand I owe you, Shylock'. 'Oh, thanks Antonio, knew you'd cough up') Shylock refuses: 'I'll have my bond; speak not against my bond . . . the Duke shall grant me justice.' In any real court the judge would then order Shylock to accept as Antonio has honoured his debt, even though a little late, Shylock would have pocketed the cash, shaken hands all round and then stalked off. As the judge nominated for the case (Portia's cousin) is ill, a substitute is called in; this is 'Dr Balthazar', actually Portia disguised as a male lawyer. She is married to Antonio's friend Bassanio which is bad news for Shylock, who does not recognise her. Portia, to give her credit, looks for a judicial way out and tries to induce Shylock to be merciful, pointing out that

> 'The quality of mercy is not strained.
> It droppeth as the gentle rain from heaven
> Upon the place beneath.'

This cuts no ice with Shylock who would agree that nobody is entitled to mercy; justice is what everyone is entitled to. He is angry that Christian Venice is denying him what is rightfully his. It is for Portia to decide the case and for the duke to pass sentence. The case was tried in accordance with Venetian law and Portia looked for a merciful solution but she concluded

> '. . . there is no power in Venice
> Can alter a decree established
> 'T would be recorded for a precedent.'

She says that she sees nothing wrong if Shylock refuses to take the money as the forfeit of flesh was agreed by both sides, and she appears to side with 'the Jew'. Shylock sharpens his knife. But, she continues, although you may take your pound of flesh you have no permission to shed one jot of blood. Shylock cannot comply with this interpretation and hesitates. He says, 'Give me my principal and let me go.' Bassanio is ready with the money but Portia intervenes again. She says that as Shylock has refused it in open court he shall have merely justice and his bond. Portia, who as a non-lawyer seems very familiar with the law, then points out that if an alien attempts to kill a Venetian, the Venetian is awarded half his property and the other half goes to the State. At one stroke she has given game, set and match to Antonio. Not only does Shylock not get back even his principal, he loses everything. As a final development Antonio forgoes his half of Shylock's wealth provided that he converts to Christianity. But in any event he keeps the three thousand ducats.

The word 'justice' occurs a lot in this short scene: the justice of an agreement the outcome over which neither side has any control; the justice of an agreement that Antonio agreed to never believing that Shylock would enforce it; the justice of taking a man's life for non-payment of a debt. Shylock's insistence that justice be upheld turns into disaster. The justice of the law of Venice is also questionable: it is one thing to deprive Shylock of his bond—even to deprive him of his principal since he has once refused it. But it is a perverted justice that results in Shylock losing everything, or losing half his wealth and his faith. In this short scene Shakespeare has demonstrated that justice is not a term that is easily understood; that it can mean different things in different circumstances to different people; and that a strict adherence to justice can easily result in injustice. The cunning and clever Portia understood what Shylock did not: we can all recognise mercy, but nobody really knows what justice really is; in this case it is perverted, with the man who forfeits his bond getting everything and the man who sought justice even if it resulted in a man's death, losing all.

The solution arrived at by Portia that Shylock can have the flesh but not the blood is a masterstroke. It is difficult to envisage a case in an English court being decided by such a clever wheeze. Where did Portia, and of course Shakespeare, get the idea from?

It is possible that he got it from the *Bible*. After the flood God rewards Noah (and his descendants) for following His instructions diligently. Up until then they were allowed to eat anything that was green, that is, vegetation. Now God says to Noah, 'Everything that lives and moves about (i.e. animals) shall be food for you' (Genesis 9:3). But you must not eat meat that has its lifeblood still in it (Gen. 9:4). And for your life blood I will surely demand an accounting (Gen. 9:5).

The trial in *The Merchant of Venice* was probably more similar to English trials in the 16th-century than to trials today. However, Shakespeare was not attempting to mimic an English court but to envisage what a perverted Venetian trial might look like and to demonstrate the difficulties that can arise with an abstract concept like justice. In many ways, however, both Shylock –'If you deny me … there is no force in the decrees of Venice' and Portia — '… there is no power in Venice can alter a decree established' — are abiding by the rules. And although Portia's solution to the impasse seems like sharp practice there is nothing morally or legally wrong about it. It is the penalties that are piled on to Shylock that are shocking. Portia could have said, 'Shylock, the law is on your side and there is nothing I can do about it. Go ahead and cut off Antonio's flesh and watch him die.' Could Shylock really bring himself to slice off the breast of a living conscious man? But that is another play.

Setting aside Berholt Brecht's play *Galileo* which includes an inquisition rather than a court trial, some four hundred years after Shakespeare, Terence Rattigan's play *The Winslow Boy* opened in 1948. The play concerns the Winslows, a rich family living in the well-off area of London, South Kensington. The father is a retired banker, his daughter is a suffragette, the elder son is at Oxford and the younger, 13-year-old son is at the Royal Naval Academy, from which he is expelled for stealing a five shilling postal order (worth about £20 today). He denies the theft to his father who hires a famous silk to take the Admiralty to court, to annul the accusation and restore his place at the academy. The family is reduced almost to penury — the son leaves Oxford, servants are dismissed — to pay for the trial (which they win), and although the court proceedings take place offstage, an interesting but little known point of law is raised. Since the Admiralty and the Crown are considered as one the Admiralty cannot be sued. To bring the Admiralty to court requires the permission of Parliament and in particular that of the Attorney General who in this play, after much shilly-shallying, grants the request.

CHAPTER 7

Trials on Television and Film

Although there have been a considerable number of films for the cinema which are centred around court trials, many of them are of American origin and since the legal system and courtroom format in the USA are different from that in Britain they will not be considered here. However, what is lacking in the cinema is relatively prolific on television screens.

One can go back forty years, to 1972, when one of the most popular and realistic courtroom dramas, *Crown Court*, was broadcast by Grenada TV. This was about as pure as courtroom fiction could get as almost the entire programme was played out in a courtroom in the fictional town of Fulchester. Each fictional case took place in three twenty-five minute episodes per week, usually on Wednesday, Thursday and Friday. The first two episodes were devoted to the prosecution case and the last to the defence. The trials were mostly for criminal offences and covered drugs, murder, arson and other serious crimes. What made the programmes even more realistic was that a real jury was drawn from people on the electoral register in an area around Granada's studios in Manchester. After each case had been presented in full, with prosecution, defence and summing-up by the judge complete, the jury was required to arrive at a verdict within thirty minutes. Only the jury could deliver the verdict and two separate endings to the final episodes were written to be relevant to whatever verdict was reached.

Many well-known and successful writers produced the scripts and well-known actors performed in many of the episodes. The series was extremely popular with the viewing public, almost certainly due to the verisimilitude of the court process, the offences tried and the real-life jury deciding the verdict; *Crown Court* lasted until 1984.

In complete contrast to *Crown Court*, a series called *Judge John Deed* was launched in 2001 and continued until 2007. This 'legal drama' featured Sir John Deed, a High Court judge. Although the series ran for six years it was heavily criticised on a number of counts. Indeed, it was probably the most criticised of all courtroom drama series. The legal profession pointed out that many of the decisions taken by Deed would never have been taken in a real court. Deed was often seen judging cases prosecuted by his ex-wife, and sometimes the defence counsel was his girlfriend. In one episode he sat on a jury and proceeded to interview witnesses. He was having an affair with his therapist. In another episode called 'Heart of Darkness' a causal link was portrayed between the MMR vaccine and autism, a link previously denied by the medical profession which criticised the programme. Any member of the public who had had no dealings with the courts, even as a spectator in the public gallery, who watched *Judge John Deed,* would have no idea what a real Crown Court was like.

The first time that TV cameras were allowed into the Old Bailey for the purpose of filming a programme, in this case a series, was in 2002 when *The Jury* first saw the light of day. The plot was that a 15-year-old boy, John Maher, had been killed by having been stabbed twenty-eight times and a Sikh classmate called Singh was charged with his murder. As the titles suggests, this series concentrates on the jury and it would challenge statistical probability if such a bizarre group of people could be drawn by chance from the electoral register. The family of the victim threaten Singh when he enters the court and later decide to influence the jurors: two imprisonable offences. One juror, Peter, tells his in-laws about the case, which at a minimum would disqualify him as a juror. Another juror receives a phone call warning her to vote guilty, whilst the defendant is abused by a prison officer. The actual trial serves as background as the complex and fairly unpleasant lives of the jurors are played out.

At the end of the trial the jury is undecided and the judge willing to accept a 10–2 majority verdict. One more juror votes not guilty and that is the verdict, since a majority of 10–2 in favour of guilty, at the judge's discretion, is acceptable for a conviction whereas a majority of 9–3 is not.

The Singh family decide to leave the country and in a bizarre ending the victim's father goes to the airport with a gun intending to kill the boy, but shoots himself instead.

A second series of *The Jury* was broadcast in 2011. The backbone of the plot was a retrial of a man convicted five years earlier of killing three women; but, as in the first series, it is the bizarre bunch of jurors—a teacher who has had an affair with a 17-year-old pupil, a man with Asperger's Syndrome, a Sudanese immigrant waiting for a USA visa—that detracts from realism.

The series had a head start as a result of the trial taking place in the real Old Bailey rather than in a mock-up court in a studio. The trials are believable and the courtroom procedure is as realistic as possible given that it is not a real trial with people coming and going, passing bits of paper and talking to each other resulting in a hubbub of background noise. If the focus of the series is the jury, as the title suggests, it is inevitable that it is not composed of twelve good men and true, leading ordinary lives, listening to the evidence and going home each evening avoiding newspapers and the *Six O'clock News*. If that were the case there would need to be at least a different title with more focus on the trial itself. But in each series the jury comprised such a weird group of people that anyone having seen the programmes and subsequently called up for jury service would have grave misgivings about their prospective colleagues; and anyone facing an imminent Crown Court trial might have serious concerns about the ability of juries to assimilate the evidence, obey the rules and arrive at a fair verdict.

Probably the most realistic trial scenes occurred in *Kavanagh QC*, a series of courtroom dramas with a star-studded cast led by John Thaw in the title role. The programmes were screened between 1995 and 2001; there were twenty-five 90 minute episodes, each telling a separate story.

The first episode, broadcast in January 1995, was called 'Nothing But the Truth'. Two young students are digging a swimming pool in a garden; one of them is called away and the other one continues. It is a hot day and around midday the lady of the house invites him in for a beer and offers him a sandwich. He is then accused of raping her and Kavanagh defends him. At trial the issue is consent. The prosecution evidence from the woman claims that the defendant, after accepting her offer of a drink proceeded to rape her. She gives an outline of the incident and prosecuting counsel explains that the victim, a youngish good-looking woman was internally examined and details are given of the results of this. The doctor's report showed no bruising to the abdomen or thighs but there were slight internal abrasions. Kavanagh's cross examination is devastating and completely ruins the prosecution version of events; so much so that in the evening Kavanagh's own daughter accused him of being too harsh.

Examined by Kavanagh, the defendant said that she told him that she and her husband were not sleeping together, and she said, 'Why don't we have some fun?' I put my hands on her breasts and she kissed me, and we ended up having sex. She asked me to be dominant, and asked if we could do it again.

The jury announce a verdict of not guilty. In the evening Kavanagh is eating in a nearby restaurant and is approached by a young girl who tells him that she is a student in the same college as the defendant. She says to Kavanagh, 'You were brilliant.' Kavanagh says that he was doing his job and she then said, 'He raped me. The man you defended is arrogant and selfish and has raped other girls in the college.' To Kavanagh's comment that she should have told him earlier and given evidence she replies, 'And have someone else tear me apart'?

When Kavanagh returns to his office later in the evening he finds the defendant there 'to thank you for getting me off.' Kavanagh tells him he has met a girl from the university and asks him to leave. He tells a colleague he had successfully defended a rapist. The colleague tells him that he had to defend him or he would have gone somewhere else. Kavanagh replies that someone else might not have got him off.

Most of the play takes place in court and the normal court procedure is followed, even to the passing of notes and whispering between counsel. Kavanagh's cross-examination of the victim and his questioning of the accused really was brilliant, and the extra twist at the end showed that even when a clever counsel 'wins' his case he can still end up with the wrong result. The rapist goes free and his victim is tarnished as a liar of loose morals.

℔

Because courts are like theatres with actors and an audience, a plot, acts, major and minor actors, and the proceedings have a beginning and an end with an either/or conclusion before everyone goes home (with the possible exception of the guilty prisoner who is taken elsewhere), it is not too diffi-cult to portray on television courtroom dramas that are realistic. However, apart from *Crown Court* and *Kavanagh* programmes were rather idiosyn-cratic: *The Jury* portrayed a fictional jury which was remote from any jury drawn from the general population, and *Judge John Deed* was frankly ridiculous. *Crown Court* had a real jury that delivered a verdict and *Kavanagh* had accurate writing and John Thaw who had made the seamless transition from Morse to Kavanagh.

In Kavanagh QC, as in other courtroom dramas, dramatic tension clearly comes from the adversarial nature of the trial. If there are not two sides in contention with each other, but the 'trial' is rather a formal investigation by a judge as, for example, the Leveson Inquiry, there may be great interest in the outcome but little or no dramatic tension. Most European countries do not have adversarial trials in which two sides—the defence and the prosecution—each state their case and challenge each other's evidence, usually represented by lawyers. There, it is the judge who does the investigation just like Lord Leveson and it is he (or she) who decides the outcome.

Although court procedure changed gradually over the centuries following the Norman Conquest in the eleventh century, and there was a slight tendency away from the judge completely running the trial—there were, for example, prosecuting lawyers—the defendant could not be represented in any meaningful way, and although a lawyer (invariably men at that time) could advise his client he could not address the prosecution or the jury, nor cross-examine the other side.

All this changed in the ten years between 1783 and 1793, and the reason for the change was the appearance on the scene of a young newly qualified lawyer called William Garrow (see *Champions of the Rule of Law*, p. 131 et seq., Hostettler J (2011), Waterside Press).

Garrow was born in 1760, admitted by Lincoln's Inn eighteen years later and called to the Bar in 1783 when he promptly began his criminal practice at the Old Bailey. At that time most crimes (felonies) carried the death sentence yet the prisoners being tried were not allowed counsel to speak on their behalf, other than on a point of law and with the permission of the judge. Nor could prisoners give evidence on their own behalf or call witnesses; an exception was that prisoners charged with high treason could engage counsel to assist them.

At the time that Garrow entered the scene some judges allowed defence counsel to cross-examine witnesses but they were not permitted to address the jury or make speeches; nor was a defendant presumed to be innocent before the trial began. Although this was pointed out by Garrow in 1791, not only was this not widely accepted but there were no rules of evidence. In short, the odds were stacked heavily against the defendants so that acquittals were relatively rare.

The slow changes towards defendants getting a fair hearing which culminated in the 1898 Criminal Evidence Act (which has since been superseded) were begun by the young fearless barrister William Garrow. He courageously attacked and exposed 'thief-takers' who were paid a substantial sum for accusing people who were subsequently found guilty. He introduced adversarial trials, argued with judges and, although forbidden to address the jury, he nevertheless did so subtly through another of his innovation, the cross-examination of witnesses which he used to devastating effect. Garrow practised at the Old Bailey for ten years and appeared in almost 1,000 trials. During that time he saved many innocent prisoners from the gallows.

Why were legal conflicts like these such a marked source of drama? It has been mentioned earlier that a court case, like a play, has three acts: the case for the prosecution, that for the defence, and the summing-up and verdict. Yet cases in Garrow's time were not like that. They were rowdy, one-sided affairs, often trivial, and the 'trial' was brief and biased towards the prosecution, the verdicts a foregone conclusion and the penalty often the gallows. Yet people packed the Old Bailey and added to the noise and rowdiness in which the proceedings were conducted. Was this really entertainment?

Theatrical performances were banned under Puritan rule. After the restoration, Charles II issued letters patent to Thomas Killigrew and William Davenant giving them a monopoly to open two theatres in London to perform serious drama as opposed to pantomime and comedies. These became the Patent Theatres. The Theatre Royal, Drury Lane, Lisle's Tennis Court in Lincoln's Inn Fields and the Theatre Royal, Haymarket were the first Patent Theatres. Other Patent Theatres, all called Theatre Royal opened in Liverpool, Bath and Bristol. The three Patent Theatres in London put on serious drama that was probably beyond the financial and intellectual reach of much of the general population. On the other hand, every day at the Old Bailey there was drama of a different kind and it was free.

This changed in 1737 when the Licensing Act restricted dramatic performances to two Patent Theatres. Censorship was tightened so that scripts had to be vetted by the Lord Chamberlain, an imposition that was repealed only as late as 1968.

This train of events was triggered by the production of a play that was a political satire called *The Golden Rump* to which Walpole took exception (was this where John Mortimer found Rumpole?) as it undermined him and the government. The play was considered obscene as it indicated that the Queen administered enemas to the King.

By the time that Garrow burst on to the scene in the late-18th century non-patent ('illegitimate') theatres were producing melodrama and burlesque shows while the legitimate, Patent Theatres produced drama.

Whereas pre-Garrow the Old Bailey resembled a rowdy house with little or no theatricality it was a form of entertainment. However, under the influence of Garrow trials became more organized, with 'parts' given to each of the two sides and to the judge and jury; they resembled plays. The rowdy forerunner provided entertainment but the adversarial trial with its three acts, and a resolution right at the end, provided drama.

Following his years at the Old Bailey Garrow entered parliament as MP for Gatton, a rotten borough. While still pursuing a successful legal career he became Solicitor General, Attorney General and a judge but in all three roles he was undistinguished; he was also made a Baron of the Exchequer thus becoming *Sir* William Garrow.

Whilst the change towards adversarial trials was honed, improved and gradually accepted in England, and adopted by many, mainly English-speaking, countries around the world, Garrow was quickly forgotten; yet thanks to him thousands of defendants in many countries have received and continue to receive a fair trial. This was the legacy that enabled programmes such as *Kavanagh QC* to be made: trials transmuted into theatre.

The evolution and establishment of adversarial trials not only offered cliff-hanging possibilities to the authors of fiction in the form of books, plays and TV programmes, but the resurrection of Garrow and his works recently spawned three series of TV plays based upon trials in which Garrow himself was engaged.

There were twelve programmes broadcast on BBC1, divided into three groups screened in 2009, 2010 and 2011. Readers interested in the minutiae of these broadcasts are advised to read *Garrow's Law*, a detailed summary and comment on every episode, by John Hostettler (2012, Waterside Press). After describing and discussing 'Garrow's gift to the world' followed by a chapter on 18th-century London life, the author turns his attention to the BBC programmes collectively called *Garrow's Law*.

In the first episode of the first series Garrow does not participate in the case—trial would be too kind a word—but observes it. A woman is convicted of stealing clothing worth more than one shilling for which she is condemned to death. Garrow shows his disgust to the solicitor to whom he had been articled before studying for the Bar, that she was not defended by counsel. This observation sets the tone for the series by highlighting a major flaw in the criminal justice system. The episode also sets the scene: an Old Bailey courtroom, noisy and chaotic, an irascible judge in charge and little justice on display: an accurate courtroom scene of the time.

Garrow's first case brings him up close to reality. He is not permitted to see the indictment against his client; he cannot see him in Newgate Prison; he can cross-examine prosecution witnesses or call witnesses as to his client's character, but they cannot be made to attend. He may not address the jury. The offence is that his client robbed a man of two shillings—a capital crime. Garrow loses it and as his client is taken away to be hanged he comments that trials should be contests with counsel available for the defence as well as for the prosecution.

After a few episodes a romantic sub-plot is introduced, possibly to lighten the unremitting flow of gloom and doom of the courtroom. The storyline explores the relationship between Lady Sarah Dore and her 'husband' Arthur Hill, Viscount Fairford. They were never married in real life but there was a child of the relationship about which little is known, so much of this episode is part fiction. What *is* known is that Sarah left Hill for Garrow who accepted Hill's and Sarah's child. All this happened some years before Garrow's arrival at the Old Bailey, when he was studying law. Much of this sub-plot is fiction although it is known that Garrow and Sarah did marry and had two children of their own and raised Hill's and Sarah's child whom Hill continued to support.

The first series of programmes was a fairly accurate depiction of a court in the Old Bailey of the period and how trials were conducted, and showed how Garrow gradually introduced a more adversarial pattern into trials, enabling him to examine his own clients in court and to address the jury. Adversarial trials were gradually being introduced.

By the end of the second series a little more fiction had crept into some episodes. In one, Arthur Hill prosecutes Garrow for 'criminal conversation' (a forerunner of the twee phrase 'intimacy took place') meaning that Garrow and Sarah had had sexual intercourse and therefore Garrow had committed adultery. However, such a trial could never have taken place since at that time Sarah and Hill were not married. The case, however, went against Garrow (on TV) and Hill was awarded 'exemplary damages' (a polite term for money) of one shilling.

The third run of TV trials followed the format of the previous two but in some of the episodes broadcast the trials had actually taken place *after* Garrow had stopped practising at the Old Bailey.

After leaving the Old Bailey and becoming an MP Garrow took other posts and was made a KC (King's Counsel), PC (Privy Councillor) and FRS (Fellow of the Royal Society). More surprisingly, he became a prosecutor and a staunch Tory. He and Sarah had their first child, David William, in 1781; Eliza Sophia was born in 1784 and Garrow and Sarah were married in 1793.

Although his glory days were over and he fulfilled his new roles indifferently, during his ten years at the Old Bailey he radically altered criminal court practice and was responsible for the introduction and evolution of adversarial trials, of defence advocates, as well as coining the phrase that has been a cornerstone of every court in the world that conducts adversarial trials: 'innocent until proved guilty'.

William Garrow died in Ramsgate, Kent on 14 September 1840.

Part 3

FORENSIC SCIENCE

CHAPTER 8

Introduction to Forensics

Before discussing how forensic science ('forensics') is portrayed in the various media and how realistic this portrayal is, it is first necessary to describe what it is and how it is used in the real world. The term covers many different disciplines. Determining cause and or time of death by body temperature or insect invasion or decomposition was used as early as the 18th-century; a number of murderers were caught and convicted using these techniques, and several pathologists, such as Sir Bernard Spilsbury became quite famous for his forensic skills. He was instrumental in the conviction of Dr Hawley Harvey Crippen having identified a small piece of skin from human remains as being from Mrs Crippen; he also played a determining part in the famous Brides in the Bath murders which was dramatised as a TV film starring Martin kemp in 2003. What is relatively new and became known as 'forensic science' was the introduction in the 20th-century of scientific methods and sophisticated technology now available for post-mortem examinations. Many branches of forensic science, such as forensic archaeology, are only rarely relevant to crime detection and seldom, if ever, appear in fiction. The general usage of the words 'forensic', 'forensics' or 'forensic science' is taken to mean scientific investigations to ascertain the cause of death or apprehension of criminals, and that is the intended meaning here.

The most common image of Sherlock Holmes is of a man in a deerstalker hat kneeling on the ground looking through a large magnifying glass. Even though Arthur Conan Doyle was a doctor and had absorbed from his mentor many of the techniques of detection due to observation and deduction, there was little else to help him: a magnifying glass, a keen eye for detail and brilliant deductive powers were all he had. Almost a hundred years later only two further helps to detection had been uncovered: fingerprints and blood groups.

Fingerprints

Fingerprints are easily deposited on to smooth surfaces by the natural secretion of sweat from the eccrine glands on the ridges of the epidermis at the fingertips. Prints from parts of the hand and even from the feet are also possible. This was noticed as early as 1665 by Marcello Malpighi at the University of Bologna. Malpighi was one of the many great Italian biological scientists as attested by the eponymous Malpighian corpuscles in the kidneys and, resulting from his fingerprint analyses, the Malpighian layer in the skin. In 1694 an English physician, Nehemiah Coln, published the first paper describing ridges on the fingers and a year later the Dutch doctor Govard Bidoo — personal physician to William III of Orange-Nassau — published a book on anatomy with illustrations of the structure of ridges on fingers. It was a German anatomist Johan Mayer who in 1788 recognised that fingerprint patterns were unique to each individual. In 1880 Henry Fauld published a paper in *Nature* discussing the usefulness of fingerprints for identification and showed how they could be recorded using printing ink.

In 1886 the Metropolitan Police dismissed the method.

Francis Galton, a cousin of Charles Dickens, analysed fingerprints and encouraged their use in forensic science in his book *Fingerprints*. He pointed out that no two people had similar fingerprints and calculated the chance of a false positive match as 1 in 60 billion. The first instance of fingerprints being used to identify a criminal was claimed to be by the French scientist Alphonse Bertillon who in 1902 found the prints on a glass showcase of the employer of the thief and murderer Henri Scheffer. Within twenty years or so fingerprint evidence, although not universally accepted, was regularly used in the detection of the identity of perpetrators of crime.

Blood groups

The use of blood found at crime scenes or on the person or clothing was made possible by the discovery by the Austrian biologist and physician Karl Landsteiner in 1900 that human blood could be divided into four categories which he names A, O, B and AB. Group O blood could be mixed with blood of any other group, but if A and B, or A and AB, or B and AB were mixed the blood clotted into clumps, rendering it unfit for transfusion. These groups were of limited use in identification since most Caucasian people had groups A and O and only a very small minority was of group B. Then in 1937, Karl Landsteiner and Alexander S Wiener discovered the rhesus factor. People either had the rhesus factor in their blood (+) or did not (-) so that the effective number of groups doubled: A+, A-, O+, O-, B+, B-, AB+, AB-. In all groups rhesus negative is less common than rhesus positive, and B- and AB- are quite rare and blood of these groups is much sought after from donors. In crime detection blood groups are useful but still limited, but a more important gain from the above classification is the ability to transfuse blood of the same group as the recipient, with the additional advantage that O+ blood can be transfused into anyone.

Although blood groups and fingerprints were the sole scientific aids to criminal investigations for almost a hundred years, in the last fifty or so forensic science has thrown up a number of aids to enable detectives to determine how victims have been injured or killed, and in many cases iden-tifying the perpetrators. Far and away the most important of these aids was a substance that had been known to exist since the middle of the 19th-century.

Deoxyribonucleic acid

Research into what became known as DNA began as early as 1868 when the Swiss biologist Friedrich Miescher studied the nuclei of pus cells obtained from used surgical bandages. He later found the same substance in the heads of salmon sperm. Although at roughly the same time a Czech monk, Gregor Mendl, using pea plants, was demonstrating how characteristics such as height and colour were inherited, the two lines of research were quite independent as Miescher and Mendl did not know of each other's existence and a further eighty or so years would pass before it became apparent that the *mechanism* for inheritance derived from the substance that Miescher partially isolated. In 1943 Avery, MacLeod and McCarty showed that DNA taken from a virulent bacterium and transferred into a non-virulent bacte-rium turned it into the virulent form. Further work by Hershy and Chase in 1952 showed that it was the DNA that provided the genetic information responsible for the replication of the virus when a bacteriophage (bacterial virus) infects a host cell (bacterium).

One of the most important biological discoveries of the 20th-century was made in 1953 by James Watson, an American geneticist and Francis Crick, a

British physicist, at Cambridge University with help from Rosalind Franklin and Maurice Wilkins at King's College, London. Watson and Crick first proposed that the structure of DNA was in the form of a double helix, and following brilliant deductive and experimental work plus Franklin's X-ray diffraction studies, produced a model of DNA. They showed that DNA consists of two helical chains coiled around the same axis in opposite directions so that each entwines the other. In 1962 Crick, Watson and Wilkins shared the Nobel Prize for Physiology and Medicine; sadly, Franklin, whose work played a key role in the discovery, had died before this date, and Nobel Prizes are never awarded posthumously.

Inside living cells DNA, usually stored in the nucleus, is arranged into chromosomes which, when a cell divides splits so that each new cell contains the same genetic material. Between 1961 and 1965 the genetic code was cracked. Further progress was made and in 1982 genetically-engineered insulin was approved for diabetics in the UK and the USA.

When DNA is isolated from living or dead tissue it has many uses in biology, biochemistry, genetic engineering, to name a few; and, of course, forensic science. Why DNA is such a useful tool for identifying or eliminating suspects, or identifying victims is that no two people in the world, not even identical twins, have the same DNA. But before DNA can be utilised as a tool it must first be extracted. This is an extremely skilled process which takes time measured in days and weeks. DNA 'profiling' was developed by the geneticist Sir Alec Jeffreys in 1984 and first used to convict Colin Pitchfork in the Enderby murders case of 1988.

DNA can be extracted from blood, semen, skin, hair or saliva and used to match the DNA of an individual. Not only is this useful in new cases but it affords the opportunity to re-examine old cases by revealing evidence that was not available at the original trial. This may result in the overturning of a guilty verdict and release from custody for someone wrongly convicted or arrested; or with inroads having been made into the double jeopardy law (see *Chapter 5*), used to provide evidence to convince a jury when the evidence at the original trial was not available. In disasters it can be used to identify victims even if they are mutilated or only body parts are available.

The procedure for the collection of samples is an art in itself and includes lifting stains on a wet swab; lifting dried blood stains with tape; scraping with a blade on to clean paper; collecting visible samples with forceps; and vacuuming dust or other detritus and storing in clean paper.

Toxic substances

Where poisoning is suspected, whether self-inflicted or by attempted or completed murder, it is important to identify the poison, quickly if the victim is still alive or more leisurely if dead. Poisons can be accumulated in urine which can be provided easily if the victim is alive. A number of drugs and toxins will be in a higher concentration in the urine than in the blood. However, a small quantity of about 10 millilitres of blood is sufficient to screen for most poisons. Some poisons find their way into the hair and because the hair is continuously growing, if a poison is administered over a period of time, analyses of different lengths of hair may indicate when the poison was administered. In Victorian times there were a number of murders involving arsenic, which migrates to the hair and a number of murderers were caught by this method. Of course, if the victim is already dead a number of varied samples may be taken, including stomach contents.

Blood splatter

When an attack on a victim results in severe bleeding the pattern the blood makes after leaving the body can yield important information to investigators about the nature of the attack and the relative positions of the attacker and the attacked when the violence was committed. Blood is a viscous liquid which after leaving the body will act like similar liquids, being influenced by gravity, viscosity and surface tension. Blood drops are spherical enabling the angle of impact to be determined when it hits a surface and splashes. This will enable the area of origin to be calculated, that is, where the victim was when attacked. This can be established more accurately if there is more than one splatter site.

Forensic pathology

There is a joke in the medical profession that says 'Physicians know what to do, but can't do it. Surgeons don't know what to do, but can do it. Pathologists know what to do and can do it; but they are too late.'

Pathologists are doctors who have specialised in anatomical pathology; they can examine tissues taken from patients in order to determine the nature of a disease, or they can perform post-mortem autopsies to ascertain the cause of death. A forensic pathologist is a pathologist who has specialised in *forensic* pathology which is the science of examining bodies or body parts in order to ascertain the cause of death where criminal activity is suspected. They may examine samples not only from the victim but also from suspects. Thus they are concerned not only with the cause of death, which is sometimes obvious, such as a bullet wound to the head, or strangulation, but will also attempt to ascertain the manner of death such as murder, accident, suicide, natural causes.

During the autopsy the forensic pathologist may attempt to determine the identity of the dead person and before invasion of the body will examine external injuries and wounds and may collect specimens of tissues and fluids for microscopic analysis. They will examine wounds or other injuries on bodies or on living patients, and collect samples that may reveal deliberate poisoning or an overdose. When there is an unexpected death they will work closely with the coroner, and if a case comes to court they may give evidence as an expert witness.

CHAPTER 9

Forensic Literature

It is not necessary to be a police officer or a criminal to write about how the police operate. Nor is it necessary to be a lawyer or a defendant to write about what happens in courts of law. But it would be extremely difficult for anybody who is not a forensic pathologist to write a novel about how forensic pathology helps with the identity of bodies or criminals or can explain the cause of death or injury. This is one reason why there are relatively few novels that hinge on the workings of forensic pathologists and those that exist are written by the same few authors. This constraint, as we shall see, does not extend to other media.

Probably the first writer to pen a full length novel centred on the work of a forensic pathologist is Patricia Cornwell, an American born in Miami, Florida in 1956. There are no major British authors whose work covers the same topic. Her first novel, *Postmortem,* was published in 1990 and won several prizes including the *Prix du Roman d'Aventure.* In this book we are introduced to Kay Scarpetta, Chief Medical Examiner to the state of Virginia, her ten year old niece Lucy who has an IQ off the scale and seems to know more about computers than Microsoft, and certainly more than her aunt; and Pete Morino, a detective sergeant whose gruff manner, dissolute appearance and grammar-free speech mask a fine deductive brain. There is also a cast of other scientific specialists who have walk-on parts.

Postmortem is obstensibly about a serial killer who enters the bedrooms of sleeping young women who are alone and then rapes, tortures and kills them. However, it is equally concerned with Scarpetta's continuing fight with some of the top brass in Virginia's government who interfere in her investigations in order to destabilise her position. It is little Lucy who works out how one of them has managed to get into Scarpetta's 'locked' computer, but neither the Medical Examiner's Department nor the police are any nearer to finding the serial rapist even after five women have been violated and killed. Breaking the unwritten rule among crime writers about the killer being mentioned early in the book, this killer is revealed only in the last few pages, and only after he has broken into Scarpetta's bedroom and been shot dead by the ever-vigilant Morino. He has not been mentioned before. Thus we are left with a book full of forensic scientists working flat out to identify the killer and failing to do so; and the killer who nobody has ever heard of being caught by a fluke in the last few pages.

Dr Cornwall has written more than 20 full length novels starring her main character Kay Scarpetta who, like Cornwell herself, is not only a senior forensic pathologist but also teaches the subject to other doctors. Cornwell has created a Chair in Organic Science at Harvard University; she has assisted in a scientific study of a Confederate submarine and in an archaeological excavation at Jamestown. She has also written eight fiction books on other subjects and five books of non-fiction. Her latest books were *Dust* published in 2013 and *Flesh and Blood* at the end of 2014.

The storylines of the Kay Scarpetta novels inevitably follow a similar pattern. Most of the action takes place in Richmond, Virginia, where Cornwell once worked. There is a suspicious death (or deaths) which are obviously murder as in *Postmortem,* or which may or may not be homicide and which has (have) stumped the local police. Scarpetta is called in and by examining the body, taking samples of organs, DNA, stomach contents and so on, solves the mystery in about four hundred pages. Although the plot outlines are similar the forensic approaches are different, the solutions being found by diverse forensic analyses. For example, in the novel *Trace* (2005) a young teenage girl has been found dead. At this time Scarpetta no longer works in Richmond but as the chief medical examiner there is unable to determine how the girl died ('There is no reason why she should be dead!') he calls in Scarpetta for help. The remainder of the book consists of descriptions of various forensic procedures resulting in her discovering the odd way by which the girl died and finally tracking down the killer as a former employee of hers who, by way of subplot, is stalking her lover and her now grown up niece Lucy.

Kay Scarpetta moves to Charleston, South Carolina, in *Book of the Dead* (2007) where she and some colleagues open a private practice that offers expert investigations and autopsies for communities that do not have these facilities. A woman is brutally murdered in her mansion home; the body of an abused young boy is found dumped in a marsh; a sixteen-year-old tennis star is found naked and mutilated. The book of the dead is actually the mortuary log. There is a great deal of scientific description in this book which many readers claimed to find difficult to understand and it received considerable criticism from reviewers.

Even with the wide range of facilities and methods available there are only a finite number of ways in which forensic scientists can do their job and Patricia Cornwall's books inevitably follow a similar pattern. Although some critics have complained that some of her books contain too much brutality, others that the science is too complicated and yet others who have said that the books have become 'much of a muchness', there has been no hint that the scientific niceties or detailed explanations are inaccurate; indeed, if there were inaccuracies only other forensic scientists would be equipped to notice them and their continued silence indicates that Cornwell's books, though they may have the defects mentioned above, are scientifically unassailable and reflect accurately how forensic pathologists work.

Although there have been a few crime writers who have dabbled at the edges of forensic science, there is only one author other than Patricia Cornwell who can lay claim to be a genuine writer of forensic science fiction, and that is Kathy (Kathleen Joan Toelle) Reichs. Kathy Reichs, a native of Chicago, is professor of forensic anthropology at the University of North Carolina at Charlotte, and spends her time between Charlotte and Montreal. She is an eminent forensic anthropologist and has been on the board of directors and vice-president of the American Academy of Forensic Science and the American Board of Forensic Anthropology. Some of her time is spent teaching Federal Bureau of Invstigation (FBI) agents how to incorporate forensic science into their methodology, and she acts as a consultant to the Chief Medical Examiner of North Carolina and to the province of Quebec. She has visited Rwanda in order to testify at the UN Tribunal on Genocide, and to Guatemala where she helped exhume bodies from a mass grave. She has also helped identify bodies and body parts of WW1 and WW2 victims as well as those resulting from the 9/11 attack on New York City. The outstanding mystery is how she has found the time to write more than twenty novels in the last seventeen years.

Whereas Cornwell's forensic pathologist Scarpetta is usually engaged in a single problem, which may have a number of side issues, Reich's forensic anthropologist, Temperance Brennan, is often working on several different problems at the same time which may or may not be connected. Her first book, *Déjà Dead* (1998) is a blockbuster of about 160,000 words; a more venal author might have made two or even three books from the intertwining storylines. The action takes place in Montreal, not a city known for its high crime rate but one very familiar to the author. The main plot is that a number of women have been killed over five or six years and have been savagely mutilated. The more recent murders have quickly come to light and the similarities of the *modus operandi* are apparent, pointing to the same perpetrator but other bodies, body parts and sometimes most of a skeleton appear. The police believe that the murders are not linked but Brennan believes that they might be. This sets up a *froideur* between her and some of the police. However, she is a forensic anthropologist and she uses all her skills to test her belief.

To state baldly that she is a forensic anthropologist is like saying that someone who can play all the instruments in an orchestra is a musician. Within her field she is a polymath. Much she can do herself: autopsies, sex and age determination from small pieces of bone. Other branches of her wide field she cannot physically perform herself as they are so specialised. but she knows precisely what she needs, who can do the science and is able to understand and interpret the results. When a body has been cut up one of her skills is to remove the flesh and examine the saw marks made on bone. She can measure the depth of indentation and the distance between the teeth but has to go to an expert in saws, describe precisely the marks she has revealed, information that enables the saw expert to indicate what type of saw was used. Her discussion with the saw expert takes several pages and the reader learns more about the different marks made by different saws than is needed for DIY. The reader also learns more about the skills available to a forensic anthropologist as eminent as Dr Reichs when she explains to the police officers in the team what she has done and what it means. Thus we learn quite a lot about the conduct of an autopsy, and a little—because it is very complex—about X-ray analysis including X-ray microfluorescence.

Reich's writing style is light despite the wince-making details of her trade and she has a penchant for similes. Many are nice as in 'appropriate' but some fall flat: 'She was thin as soup in a homeless shelter' is a total mismatch. But one cannot be but awed by the well-explained science that is on almost every page; and if she has written anything that is wrong there are very, very few people who would notice; but then in real life there are few as eminent in her field as she.

In *Grave Secrets* (2002), for example, she is mostly in Guatemala where she is helping in a mass grave exhumation and examining the remains, often the skeletons, of bodies, some of which have been dead for a number of years, others less so, which had been dumped in a septic tank where they had disintegrated, resulting in unusual and different problems. At the same time she is trying to trace the fate of a number of young girls who have disappeared, including the daughter of the Canadian ambassador, who, it is gradually revealed, has a soft spot for the ladies, unbecoming to a senior diplomat. His daughter is missing, her mother is distraught and the girl is eventually found not in a Guatemalan grave but shoplifting in Montreal.

Patricia Cornwell's forensic problems are mostly concerned with cause of death and identification of the killer, and have a relatively low body count. The forensic pathologist is mostly concerned with trace items found on or in the body or in the vicinity of where it is found. Because of the precise details of the science and the minute amount of substance with which she has to work it is often difficult to understand what she is doing and why; and she does it mostly by herself aided by skilled technicians. She is single-minded and apart from occasional references to her niece to whom she is devoted, and to a lover who lives many miles away, she is very self-contained.

Kathy Reich's forensic anthropologist, just as gifted in her field, is a more rounded character. Her investigations are often complex and, without help, difficult to understand. But Temperance Brennan is more reader-friendly; when she is about to embark on a complicated forensic investigation, by explaining to a colleague or a reporter or to a relative of a missing person what she is about to do and why she is doing it, and then explaining what she has done, what she has discovered and what it means. The reader is enabled to understand the process as it unfolds, not, perhaps, the detailed science but the general direction of her investigation and analyses. Brennan is not a loner as Scarpetta tends to be, and although she obviously understands the many aspects of the methodology, she makes no pretence at being able to do it all by herself, but engages other experts to do CAT scans or analyse cat hair, identify DNA samples, or identify the mother of foetal bone particles. Although she is an expert in her field to whom all her colleagues and assistants look up, she is also rather 'girly': she is attracted to two detectives, one Guatemalan and the other Canadian, uses make-up and perfume, and the clothing she changes into after a day's work with disintegrated bodies is often described—even her choice of underwear.

Bones to Ashes (2007) is not only a gripping read but also an education. It concerns the search for her friend and her friend's sister who mysteriously disappeared when she was about twelve-years-old; and also the quest to tally skeletons with missing persons (MPs) and skeletons and bodies found often by chance (DOAs: dead on arrival). Reichs employs a considerable array of forensic techniques, each appropriate to the type of problem the body or body part presents. Her heroine, Temperance Brennan, cannot do everything herself, nor can she distribute jobs to skilled technicians as Scarpetta does. But she has a network of expert scientists, not all pathologists, whom she employs on an ad hoc basis. In the course of the book, because the expert has to explain to Brennan what can be done and the methodology, as in other books the reader learns something of the various techniques employed. There is also a three page explanation of leprosy—how it is passed on, the symptoms, the treatment; and a fascinating explanation by a linguistic analyst who explains why he has come to the conclusion that two poems, written decades apart, were by the same person.

An extra attribute is that the books are very well written and Reichs has a feel for language that has undoubtedly developed over the years, which is not all that common among scientists, not even scientists who write books. Who but a fine writer could write a sentence such as 'All laughter fled when leukaemia conquered Kevin' with its internal alliteration and scanned rhythm. Her similes are better too: 'The next day dawned as if auditioning for a travel brochure'. The quality of the writing enables the reader to make sense of something that most readers do not encounter: forensic anthropology.

CHAPTER 10

Forensic Plays

There are really no theatrical productions that illustrate the work of forensic scientists. This is hardly surprising: it would be difficult enough to convert a stage into various scientific laboratories but to depict on stage a mortuary with bodies being cut up and organ samples being taken would be nigh on impossible. Dummies could be used but would look silly.

However, there is one play that does not depict forensic science but there is a high body count, two female murderers, the audience knows who the murderers are throughout and the murderers get away with it. This play is not a taut drama; there are thirteen murders; the victims are all elderly men; the murders are not investigated; the victims are not missed and the audience is rolling in the aisles with laughter. The play is a farce and it is called *Arsenic and Old Lace.*

This play was written by Joseph Kesselring and was performed in New York City in 1941 and 1942. It was later made into a film starring Cary Grant. It is virtually impossible to describe a farce in ordinary prose but, briefly, the action takes place in the Brewster household which is occupied by mad people. The two aunts, Abby and Martha, dominate the household and regularly murder elderly gentlemen 'who have nothing to live for' by offering then a glass of home-made elderberry wine laced with a cocktail of poisons. Teddy, who thinks he is Teddy Roosevelt, spends much of his time in the cellar where he is 'digging a lock for the Panama Canal'; his digging is useful for burying the bodies produced by his two aunts. So far there are twelve victims, all safely buried in the cellar. Among other crazy characters are Jonathan and his normal brother Mortimer who is with his new bride Elaine. Arrangements are made to have Teddy committed and to be transferred to Happy Vale. One morning the superintendent of this asylum, Mr Witherspoon, arrives with all the committal papers to be filled out. It is morning and the aunts offer him breakfast. He politely declines and points out that as superintendent he is obliged to keep to the formalities. He is offered a glass of wine and declines this too, but the ladies tell him that it their own home-made elderberry wine and not wishing to be impolite he accepts. He takes the glass and stands up to deliver a toast. There follows one of the most famous stage directions of the theatre, which ends the play:

Witherspoon toasts the ladies and lifts the glass to his lips, but the curtain falls before he does…

There are a few other plays in which characters are poisoned, though not on such a scale, and they too have only a slight brush with forensic science. But none are so hilarious as *Arsenic and Old Lace* nor do they have a comparable body count. The play is full of crazy people, many not mentioned above, doing crazy things but like all good farces the plot is ruthlessly logical.

CHAPTER 11

Forensic Films and Television

The term 'forensic' applied to films is rather a loose usage of the word. There are a number of films listed under this heading and one can even Google 'forensic films', but what is called forensic are fingerprints, blood groups, a few hairs: all the items that used to be called clues. They portray nothing comparable to what Patricia Cornwell and Kathy Reichs write about. There are no portrayals of real forensic pathologists doing forensic pathology. In one film, *The Bone Collector*, a scrap of paper, ground oyster shell, a cow hair and some asbestos are found, not in the same place. This is the stuff of Sherlock Holmes, not forensic pathology. In *Murder by Numbers,* which to be fair is labelled a psychological thriller, the main character is 'interested in forensics' and uses this interest to commit murder. If one reads through the readily available synopses of 'the five (or ten) best forensic films' there is nothing in these summaries that merits the adjective 'forensic'. Certainly, to identify a hair as cow hair, comparing bullets, or fine particles as oyster shell is clever; but it is the sort of thing that would occupy a forensic scientist little time.

Television, on the other hand, has thrown up a number of series that can unequivocally be labelled 'forensic', where the main interest of the story is how the forensic scientist goes about his or her business and solves the problem. Indeed, television is an ideal medium for depicting the role of forensic pathology in solving crime. Enough detail can be shown without it becoming too gruesome, and as much explanation given to suit a mixed audience, neither too scientifically complex nor offensively simplistic.

Probably the first TV series that portrayed forensic science as its central *motif* was *Quincy ME.* ME stands for medical examiner, the American term for forensic pathologist. The series ran from 1976 to 1983 on NBC and starred Jack Klugman as Dr Quincy. Whereas early episodes were more concerned with criminal investigations and crime solving using forensic know-how, later series brought in themes of social responsibility, in which Klugman himself was interested. The themes were wide-ranging and included drunken driving, poor plastic surgery, hazardous waste and the widespread ownership of handguns. The programmes depicted proper forensic examinations and analyses for the first time, although in the 1970s and early-1980s many of the technical advances that have made forensic pathology such a vital tool today had not yet been discovered or developed. Although the science depicted then was fairly elementary compared with today's methodology, there was nothing wrong with it: it was accurate.

CSI: Crime Scene Investigation, another American series began in 2000 and continued for more than twelve years. Events took place in Las Vegas and were based on the importance of evidence. Among the scientists were a blood pattern analyst, a technical analyst, a medical examiner and a scientist who was both a toxicologist and a DNA technician.

The first British series based on the solving of crime by means of forensic science was *Silent Witness*. The series, which was first broadcast in 1996, was devised by a former murder squad detective who had worked in Nottingham. The programme was based on a real forensic pathologist from Sheffield, Professor Helen Whitwell. Her fictitious counterpart was Professor Sam Ryan who was played by Amanda Burton until 2004. Her post was filled by her senior assistant who was promoted to professor. A new member of the team, Dr Nikki Alexander who had worked in pathology in South Africa for six months but was certified to practise: not exactly a Scarpetta or a Brennan.

The programme consisted of a series of two part episodes. The rather clever title referred, of course to a dead body, at least one of which was central to the plot, and the pathological investigation that exposed it as the silent witness to the crime. Among other countries it was broadcast in Sweden under the title of *Tyst Vittne,* which is an exact translation, and in Norway *Tanse Vitner*, Silent Witnesses, which is probably more accurate.

The depictions of the scientific aspects of the investigations were mostly pathological, far more like those of Cornwell than of Reichs, but there is always a police presence in every episode. In 2012 the programme was criticised for being 'unduly gruesome', which is presumably a notch above merely gruesome, and also too violent. The BBC responded that any violence and gruesomeness was implicit rather than depicted, that the show is after the nine o'clock watershed; and that great care is taken to avoid upsetting the audience. They did not point out that forensic pathology and autopsies are not everybody's taste and that one could always switch off.

The lack of reality also came in for some criticism. In an interview by Laura Barnett in *The Guardian* of 9 January 2011, the unnamed interviewee, presumably a forensic pathologist, began by saying of *Silent Witness* that 'This programme bears as much resemblance to reality as a badger does to a stealth bomber', a baffling simile that could have come straight out of one of Kathy Reichs' early books. 'We are only human,' she continues, and '…the last thing we do is get all woe-is-me about it.' She contrasts the 'flash laboratory' of the programme with the mortuaries where she presumably worked that date back to Victorian times. The interviewee 'tends' to remove organs from the torso 'in one go' but in the programme hearts and livers are removed individually, apparently to enhance the shock to the viewers. 'I'm not stupid,' she asserts temptingly, 'I know this show is more about entertainment. But I do think it's quite damaging.'

However, the series has a medical consultant, a real forensic pathologist who advises on the accuracy of what is depicted, and presumably the programme makers take his advice. If any criticism can be levelled at the programmes it is that they are too successful: week after week, one or more bodies, autopsies, a bit of science and the bodies are identified, the cause of death determined and the perpetrator, if there is one, arrested. But it must be realised if the programme regularly showed dead people being cut up to no avail very few people would bother to watch.

If *Silent Witness* was mostly about autopsies and attendant pathology with a few policemen thrown in, *Waking the Dead* was basically a police thriller with scientific help. The pilot episode was broadcast in September 2000; the stories are split into two episodes each lasting one hour and shown on consecutive days. Central to the programme was a cold case unit run by CID police officers headed by Detective Superintendent Peter Boyd played by Trevor Eve, aided by a forensic scientist and a profiler. They investigate, and solve, old cases with the help of new evidence recently come to light and techniques that were not available at the time the crimes were committed. After nine series Trevor Eve announced that this would be his last, and rather than seek a new central character to replace him the BBC closed the series.

In the pilot episode the cold case unit was set up and its first case concerned the murder of a young girl whose body had been found mutilated, naked, raped and battered five years earlier, but the trail had gone cold after three weeks. That this case had been re-opened triggered the murderer to kidnap another young girl who had gone missing and it was recognised that the two cases were possibly linked and would be examined together. The episode was dominated by police activity and towards the end lots of police cars racing around with lights flashing and sirens wailing. The input from the forensic expert and the profiler was minimal and fairly trivial. The pathologist discovered fibres at the scene where the first girl was found and said that they may have come from a carpet. The profiler indicated that the kidnapper did not intend to kill. He was in his twenties and enjoyed what he was doing. How she intuited this was not explained. Later in the programme Boyd asked her what she knew. She replied that she did not *know* anything but was indicating what was likely from her profiling. The pathologist looked at two letters sent by the perpetrator(s) and asserted that they were written by the same person. When they were in the building where the first girl had been kept prior to her murder the pathologist used a large scraper to remove paint or distemper off a wall in two places to reveal large blood splashes. She tells her colleagues that 'He must have hit her with something quite bulky' which, considering her head had been bashed in in two places, was hardly news.

The episode ends with the police offering to pay a ransom to be delivered by a WPC. However the murderer wants to avenge Boyd for reopening the case of the five year old murder and she is herself taken prisoner. Several police car chases later she is rescued moments before being macerated at a waste disposal dump and the murderer is captured. The pathologist plays no further part but during the police interview with the arrested man profiling comes to the fore and it is established that because the murderer's mother was not nice to him, often keeping him in a dark room, he embarked on a career of kidnapping, rape and murder.

What is clear from this pilot is that the profiler, with great authority, comes out with these gems which are nothing more than glorified guesswork and that the forensic pathologist, who looks young enough to be on work experience, can do anything from fibre analysis, DNA-testing and handwriting comparisons. The police are like real police, but the 'scientists' bear little resemblance to real scientists. As the various series progressed personal issues were introduced, presumably to make the characters more rounded. Boyd became more angry and irascible, the profiler, Grace, suffers from cancer; and social issues such as child abuse, war crimes and racism were introduced into the plots.

In July 2004 an episode entitled 'In Sight of the Lord' was screened which introduced religion into the plot. It is a most complex tale with a large number of characters and many time shifts. It begins in 1948 when a woman is startled from her sleep by a loud noise. She goes down to the kitchen where she finds her husband George dead on the floor with a nine inch nail driven through his skull. The scene shifts to the present day when his grandson makes a TV appeal for someone to solve the murder. After that it is rather like *Die Fledermaus*: once the overture ends the rest is completely incomprehensible. In 1958 George's wife falls in front of a train and her death is taken as suicide. This cold case comes to the attention of Boyd and co and the police find the body of a seventy-year-old man, badly decomposed, with a nine inch nail through his skull. Frankie, the pathologist does not believe that it was the nail that killed him but that he was already dead. A man named Joe Brackely arrives at the office and explains that he was a close friend of the dead man, William Davis, even though they lived many miles apart. The confusion grows and so do the 'findings' of the pathologist Frankie and the profiler, Grace.

Frankie disagrees that the use of nine inch nails could have a sexual meaning and after trying to read a letter written in 1944 under a microscope decides it is about a secret. Grace goes beyond her remit and finds a case going back to 1961 where a man named Norman Taylor was killed by a nine inch nail through the skull. Frankie announces that Davis died of a heart attack which is a pretty clever finding from a badly rotted corpse with a nail through his skull. Davis' former wife Carmen and her daughter Sophie are located. They are devout Christians.

More characters are introduced adding to the confusion of the team and no doubt the audience too. One of the junior police officers in the team, Mel, not Frankie the pathologist, makes a cast of a hole in the floor at the working men's drinking club and concludes that the nails used on each of the three dead men were forged from the same lot; and she also found brain tissue.

The profiler arranges a meeting with Sophie, Davis' daughter. She tells Grace that she fell in love with an older man, became pregnant, discovered that her lover was her brother and had an abortion. God would punish her. Later Frankie runs DNA tests and established that Sophie's lover was not her brother after all. Nonetheless Sophie has been naughty enough to warrant God's punishment.

Whatever one may think of the plot summary is not relevant here. What does become clear, and even clearer if the entire show is watched, is that the young forensic pathologist can do with great speed what would normally take a whole team of specialists days if not weeks to carry out, all with a minimum of equipment in a small laboratory. The profiler, Grace, delivers her opinions as gospel: there cannot be a copycat killer because the killing is personal. Whereas the portrayal of the police is realistic that of the scientific back-up is not. In some instances it is laughable.

A later episode of *Waking the Dead* illustrates that although the police and the pathologists change, the plots are still complex and intriguing but that the scientific background is still unreal. 'The Fall' was shown in January 2007. The opening scene, with no dialogue, shows a youngish woman leaning over her sleeping husband and kissing him on the lips and leaving. We follow her through the streets by taxi and on foot and see her enter the building partially occupied by a bank in the City. She enters a room where her lover works and the scene cuts to their having sex with her sitting on a table facing the camera and only her lover's back is visible held in place by her arms. The door opens quietly and the husband appears. He silently removes a gun from his pocket, raises it and just as the woman spots him, shoots the man in the back and they both topple off the table, both dead.

Some fifteen or so years later, when the bank building is derelict and being renovated, the bodies are discovered, partially decomposed and partially mummified, having fallen through the floor, but still 'sexually conjoined' as the forensic pathologist announces. Passports and airline tickets are found with the obvious implication, and the cold case team who visit the site conclude that the couple were having sex prior to running off together when a single bullet killed them both.

The pathologist becomes very busy. Before sex, the couple celebrated their imminent departure with champagne. A broken glass is found and is tested for DNA. She then performs an autopsy on the tangled bodies and without untangling them announces the height of each: five feet eleven for the man, and five feet eight for the woman. She then takes fingerprints and carries out a fingerprint check and finally, and even more remarkably given that there is a single bullet and two twisted bodies knotted together that had fallen through the floor, works out the trajectory of the bullet and the place from where the gun was fired.

From this point on the plot becomes more complicated; the dead man was identified as a securities trader who was under investigation for insider dealing, and the woman was a financial journalist who had uncovered previous financial scandals. Later on, the religious order Opus Dei was also implicated. Once again the activities of the police are plausible but the accompanying science is not.

Part 4

A SUMMING UP

CHAPTER 12

Conclusions

It should be borne in mind that when people write novels, short stories, plays, films or television shows they have a number of aims but one aim is important above all: entertainment. Crime writers are writing stories, not treatises on the work of the police. Writers of courtroom dramas are not writing about the intricacies of criminal litigation but about a series of events that can end in only one of two ways. Writers of crimes whose solutions depend on forensic pathology have a difficult task: to devise a plot that is solved by the application of scientific method, to work out how the criminals can be caught by the use of a variety of scientific techniques, and—hardest of all—to write in such a way that the public can understand what the scientists are doing; all while making gruesome images entertaining.

And overarching all these requirements is the need to create their product in a way that will prompt the public to buy the books, visit the theatre and cinema, and switch on the telly. In order to be in with a chance of influencing the public to do these things their products must not only be enjoyable but also believable. There is little point in producing a well-written and entertaining piece if the plot has no more credibility than a fairytale. Such products do occur: the books end up in charity shops at 10p each, the plays close after five performances and the TV shows are pulled after the critical response to the pilot. Even farces, particularly farces, have to be believable whilst they are being watched and the various actions must click together like a piece of machinery, which is why *Arsenic and Old Lace* has been included. Every crazy action contributes to a total shambles, but each separate action is not only believable but often inevitable and anticipated by the audience. This requires writing of the highest order.

Sometimes these requirements are conflicting and have to be interpreted widely. Nobody could suggest that *Crime and Punishment* is an 'entertaining' read, but it entertains in a different way from *The Pickwick Papers*. *King Lear* and *Antigone* are brutal plays; they are entertaining but not in the same way as *Much Ado About Nothing* or *Charley's Aunt.* Musical comedies such as *South Pacific* or *Top Hat* entertain, but not in the same way as *Tosca* or *The Magic Flute.* Each half of the above pairs will attract a different audience and readership but will entertain in their own way. *Crime and Punishment* and *Antigone* are serious works designed to illustrate how humans behave in certain circumstances: they have an intention beyond mere entertainment. *Top Hat* and *Pickwick Papers* intend to make people chuckle or leave the theatre happy. When reading or watching — and especially when criticising — it is important to recognise what the author is trying to get across.

The Police in Literature

From Edgar Allan Poe and Arthur Conan Doyle to Minette Walters and Reginald Hill the public's demand for crime novels and stories has been insatiable. There is a fascination with the criminal mind and activities, and the workings of the police. Criminal activity is endlessly ingenious whereas police activity changes slowly with evolving tools such as fingerprinting and DNA. The early books, and tales set in the mid-20th-century, usually had a lone crime solver such as Christie's Poirot or Marple, Allingham's Lugg, and Sayers' Lord Peter Wimsey. None of them had anything to do with the police, or if they occasionally interacted with them it was only to demonstrate how stupid the police were compared with the lone private detective.

These books and short stories were, and still are, immensely entertaining, but they are quite remote from reality. It is true that Poe's Dupin and Conan Doyle's Holmes operated when the role of the police was to keep the peace and prevent crime, not solve it. To that extent the detective tales were fairly true to life although the success rate of these private sleuths was undoubtedly exaggerated: they were never defeated. How could they be? Nobody would want to read a story or novel whose conclusion is that the detective has no idea who the criminal is. The single private eye gradually morphed into the single detective: a police officer who belonged to a police force but worked largely on his or her own, a 'private' detective but employed by the police. P D James' Adam Dalgleish and Ruth Rendalls' Inspector Wexford fall into this category. They are borderline insofar as there probably are gifted detectives working in police forces, who are given a great deal of rope and have a high success rate. And in the late 20th and early 21st-entury we can read about Hill's Dalziel and Pascoe who are employed by the police and use other members of the police area; but the crimes are solved by one or both of the two CID specialists.

Colin Dexter's character Inspector Morse was the archetype of police officer playing private detective. He and his side-kick Sergeant Lewis work within a police force in Oxford and although they do occasionally use the services provided by the police force to which they are attached they act mostly as if they were engaged in some private pursuit of criminals. Although very readable, and the TV series very watchable, the antics of these two police officers are far from realistic.

To sum up, it would appear that for about a hundred and fifty years crime novels about detection bear little relation to how the police actually work. But few would doubt their ability to entertain, and the quality of the writing, though variable, was generally of a high standard.

The Courts in Literature

The quality of books about court proceedings varies enormously. Agatha Christie's short story *Witness for the Prosecution*, though very famous, was made into a play and then a full length film, was not very good, particularly in terms of its closeness to real life. Its fame derives from its twist at the end but the bulk of the story is very contrived, the famous twist particularly. But it is what goes on in court, at her husband's trial for murder, that is so unreal as she is a witness not for her husband's defence but for the prosecution. His wife who, we learn late in the story, was an actress, invents a scenario quite at odds with what actually happened, a bundle of lies that gets her husband off, followed by a later admission to her counsel that he was guilty all along. This is a good example of a tale that is entertaining, is believable at first reading, but where the contrivances, revealed before the end, would not stand up in a real court.

Fletcher's *The Judge Corroborates* is quite far-fetched. The actual story is entertaining and intriguing until the judge conducting a trial for attempted burglary learns that the burglary was to take place at his own home and that the would be burglars already had it staked out. Had such a remarkable event taken place in a real court the judge would have stopped the trial and ordered a re-trial in front of another judge. But this judge joins in and his interventions lead to the longstanding burglars being acquitted.

The nicest thing that can be said about Kevan's *Law and Peace* is that it is a playful romp. It is far more about a barristers' chambers than either the law or the courts. There was probably no intention to make the events seem realistic, nor are they.

When stories and novels are written by real lawyers about the law and the courts the level of quality is raised many notches, as illustrated by the works of John Mortimer and Henry Cecil.

Mortimer is famous for his character Horace Rumpole, 'Rumpole of the Bailey', an elderly experienced barrister, whose legal career is fleshed out by various intrigues within his chambers and his liking for red wine that seems to exceed his liking for his wife Hilda. Mortimer allows himself considerable leeway when Rumpole is in court, always acting for the defence. His trials run strictly according to protocol: he makes no attempt to derive extra humour by diverting from a realistic portrayal of a court or the procedure therein. But he does take liberties with repartee between Rumpole and the presiding judge, employing dialogue that would never take place in a court of law. But then Mortimer makes no secret that his writing is meant to be humorous and if he swerves a little from realism, so be it; his books are always entertaining, popular and many of his tales have been adapted for television.

Henry Cecil is different from Mortimer in a number of ways. His writing has greater finesse and is more literary. He writes both novels and short stories and many of the short stories have nothing to do with the law and are quite far ranging in subject matter. Many are very short and he has a taste for the twist in the tale. In many ways he is a latter day O Henry. In regard to his novels and stories that are concerned with the law he keeps strictly within the limits of reality. There are occasions in his stories where there is a conflict between counsel and judge (he has the advantage of having been both) and although the judge always has the last word, as he must, the verbal exchanges are always realistic and conducted with the politesse and decorum associated with lawyers in court. Finally, many of his legal stories are very instructive, not only for their verisimilitude but also because he often writes about the minutiae of the legal processes and the more abstruse aspects of the law. His work is always entertaining and more cerebral than that of other writing on similar subjects, but the entertainment is derived from wit rather than from jokes and produces a wan smile rather than a belly laugh.

To sum up, stories based on law courts, lawyers, judges and court cases that do not hold the attention and entertain must be badly written indeed. There is a wide range of courtroom books both in subject matter and quality. Like all writing some is better than others; the problem for non-lawyers is that they often tend to stray from a realistic portrayal of what actually goes on and is said in court. Many readers do not notice this drift from reality and their enjoyment is unimpaired, but for some it may produce a gnashing of teeth. It depends upon the quality of the work in other respects whether a departure from protocol annoys, but it is fair to say that when the work is by lawyers such as Mortimer's rumbustuous Rumpole and Cecil's miniature marvels, there is little to complain about.

Forensics in Literature

There are many lawyers who write fiction concerning the law, courts and trials; there are many non-lawyers who know enough about the law — or think they do — to write stories with a legal theme. Hence libraries are full of novels and volumes of short stories concerned with the law.

There are far fewer pathologists than there are lawyers. Moreover, there are even fewer forensic pathologists and it would be nigh on impossible for a person who was not a forensic pathologist to write novels where the plot depends on a forensic pathologist/anthropologist/archaeologist/entomologist carrying out the work of his or her profession. Thus there are only two important writers in the highly specialised field, both American women and each eminent in her profession even before putting finger to keyboard.

Dr Patricia Cornwell and Dr Kathy Reichs are forensic pathologists each with a different speciality who over and above their professional work have written almost fifty novels between them in which their own areas of expertise play a salient role in the plots. They each have a different and distinctive writing style and it would probably be more difficult for either of them to describe procedures that are false than those that are true. Although Kay Scarpetta and Temperance Brennan are imaginary 'superwomen' they are probably no better at their jobs than their creators. Whatever criticisms one may have of their work — too gruesome, too similar, too complicated, etc. — the one thing that the reader can be sure of is that the science is realistic.

Police in the Theatre

Very little in the theatre is realistic and one cannot blame theatrical productions for that. The skill of the theatre is in creating a false, unreal situation that will illustrate a real one: telling lies to reveal the truth. How can one do that in a few square yards of empty space, in a couple of hours? Shakespeare knew the problem. Jacques, the sad clown in *Much Ado About Nothing,* says (Act II, Scene vii), 'All the world's a stage and all the men and women merely players'. That may be where Shakespeare found his inspiration, but presenting his ideas had greater problems. He needed

> 'A Kingdom for a stage, princes to act,
> And monarchs to behold the swelling scene!'

But Shakespeare had to be content with 'this unworthy scaffold', but asks

> 'Can this cockpit hold
> The vasty fields of France? Or may we cram
> Within this wooden O the very casques
> That did affright the air at Agincourt?'

He had none of the fancy technology we see in theatres today. There was no revolving stage, clever lighting, artistic scenery and comfortable air conditioned auditoriums that we now take for granted. He did not need them. His audience, mostly standing around his wooden O, were mesmerised by the most wonderful language ever to be uttered on our planet. The real Agincourt is a just a small stretch of land with a few cattle, but on the 'unworthy scaffold' it becomes a place where 'Yon Island cattle, desperate for their bones, ill-favor'dly become the morning field'.

Even Shakespeare would have had a tough time writing plays involving the police, though he did well enough with soldiers. Modern dramatists realise that there are better media than the stage for police drama. Where the police have been involved, in Christie's *The Mousetrap*, Stoppard's *The Real Inspector Hound* or Priestley's *An Inspector Calls* the 'police' are totally unreal, nor are they the main characters, but the plays are none the worse for that.

Courts in the Theatre

The Bard could have fitted a courtroom into his wooden O, and of course, he did. Who can equal the trial scene in *The Merchant of Venice* for sheer edge-of-your-seat drama? There have been 'trials' such as the trial of Joan of Arc in Bernard Shaw's *St Joan*, but apart from adaptations from books (Christie's *Witness for the Prosecution*}, nothing of any note. The theatre does not lend itself to such a static depiction and playwrights have avoided the subject.

One exception to this is Arthur Miller's *The Crucible.* This was not included in the above section concerning theatre and courts, as it is not only American but contains a trial that took place in the 17th-century and was based on a belief in witches and other magic. Miller consulted the archives in the town of Salem, Massachusetts, as his starting point, and demonstrated how a trial based on hearsay, false witness and unsubstantiated evidence can ruin lives even without a death sentence (which Salem had). The men in charge of the running of the trials already knew what the outcomes would be. Just like McCarthy and his House Committee on Un-American Activities.

Forensics in the Theatre

Probably the most ghoulish scene in the theatre — even worse than Shylock's near miss — occurs in *King Lear* when the Duke of Gloucester has his eyes gouged out by Cornwall: 'Out vile jelly' (Act III, Scene vii). This action never loses its horror even for those who have seen the play many times. How much more chilling would be the depiction on the stage of an autopsy, say, or the examination of decayed human remains? Of course, the actual deed could be omitted with the pathologist left to describe the forensic procedure, but unless in the hands of a master, this would not make much of a play. Consequentially playwrights, even masters, have avoided this topic.

Police on TV and in Films

The above media are ideal for full length films or episodes concerned with the police. The early radio or TV programmes, such as *PC 49*, *Dixon of Dock Green* and the feature film *The Blue Lamp,* did not at all reflect the real police and their activities but fairly accurately did reflect the public's perception of the police: kindly men who helped you across the road, told you the time and occasionally stumbled on a crime being committed with a friendly ''ullo,

'ullo, 'ullo' which quickly diffused the situation, sent the would be criminal on his or her way, and the viewers to bed with a cup of cocoa.

Times changed, society became rougher and so did the police. This was reflected in the media with programmes such as *Z Cars, The Sweeney, Special Branch* and *The Bill*. These programmes illustrated the tough side of the police racing around in squad cars, chasing criminals, arresting some; there was barely a mention of the other side of the police work, the social service side. Only *The Bill*, which ran for a long time, showed life in a police station as well as police out of it and was probably the most realistic, if not the most exciting, police programme of all.

Courts on TV and in Films

Courtroom dramas are very popular because that is what trials are: dramas. They take place in what is a glorified theatre; there is an easily understood theme; there are goodies and baddies; there are two sides; there is a dramatic climax; there is a resolution; and sometimes there is a frisson of excitement: the sentence. However, they are not all good, either as entertainment, although that is personal, or as a realistic presentation of a court. The majority of the population have never seen the inside of a courtroom unless as a defendant, witness or juror so are not aware of how realistic or not the drama is.

The early programme *Crown Court* was pure courtroom fiction. The court looked realistic, the proceedings took several days in small chunks, and there was a real jury made up of local inhabitants who delivered the verdict. It was really as good a representation as could be expected, on a small scale.

Judge John Deed, on the other hand, was the opposite: a pastiche of how a court operates and how those within it behave. Anybody unacquainted with courts would learn nothing from this programme full of lawyers and the judge behaving in ways that no lawyer would ever behave and saying things that no lawyer would say.

The Jury had a head start by being filmed in the real Old Bailey. It was an unusual twist to focus on the jury rather than on the defendant and the barristers. However, the jurors were so unusual and their behaviour so bizarre that one quickly lost all sense of reality. It would be extremely unlikely to draw randomly from the surrounding population such an unusual and unlikable group of people to deliver a verdict on some unfortunate defendant.

Kavanagh QC had the best of all worlds; in addition it had John Thaw in the title role. The courtroom looked like a courtroom, the barristers looked and talked like barristers, even passing little notes and whispering, the judge was usually fair and sometimes stern; altercations between judge and counsel were conducted politely, and the storylines were engaging. If you like this sort of thing then this is the sort of thing you'd like. Anybody disappointed by the end of the series should visit their local Crown Court. It is open most weekdays, it is free and the cases are very varied. And everyone is real.

Forensics on TV and in Films

Apart from a few films derived from books there are no films whose main themes are concerned with forensic pathology. But this is not the case with television.

Medical type programmes are very popular with the public but they usually prefer the main characters alive; when the star of the show is dead and decaying it has limited appeal. The earliest programme of its kind, *Quincy ME* avoided the most stomach churning depictions of death and Jack Klugman himself was very watchable. The British version, *Silent Witness* pulled few punches and post-mortems were all the rage. The star, pathologist Sam(antha) Ryan was very much a clever dick who specialised in examining bodies to find out what had happened to them, often to solve a murder.

Waking the Dead was different; it was essentially a police drama involving a cold case unit with a pathologist and a profiler thrown in. The plots were often quite complex and sometimes difficult to follow: a difficulty exacerbated by there being always two and often more time zones being depicted. The three main characters were also somewhat odd. The detective superintendent, Peter Boyd, was very much on the ball and a real leader, but given to violent fits of temper. The profiler, Grace, 'profiled' in such details from so few facts that one was reminded of fairground fortune tellers. And the pathologist, who changed during the series, was usually a fairly young girl who was apparently talented in all branches of pathology, chemistry, haematology, graphology and DNA-analysis so that one expected her at any time to come up with the winner of the 2.30 at Doncaster.

Afterthoughts

It is clear from the foregoing that the producers of crime fiction, whatever the medium, whether it be stories, books, plays on the stage or films on the big screen or on TV, the stories, plots or characters are not really true to life. Members of the public acting alone do not solve crimes and bring criminals to justice. Clever young girls (or boys) are not able to use the whole gamut of forensic technology alone in an area the size of an average kitchen. So as well as examining how true to life written crime novels portray the police or how realistic pathologists are in a TV series featuring dead bodies, let us look at how accurate stories, plots or characters are when represented in the various media.

It all began with crime stories. A crime is presented to the reader; the crime seems difficult or impossible to solve; the hero of the story solves the crime and the criminal is brought to justice.

Crime stories began with Edgar Allan Poe in the middle of the 19th-century. Why, in *The Murders in the Rue Morgue*, did he invent a detective (as we now know them) acting alone? The answer is simple: at the time he wrote the tale there were no police, or at least, police as we know them. The first police force in the USA was formed in 1844 and a few other forces were formed in the following few years. The intention was for them to replace the vigilante system whereby the recent immigrants from Ireland and Germany, whose behaviour was considered unacceptable, would be controlled by the previous immigrants from England and The Netherlands.

Poe's first story, about the *Rue Morgue* murders, was published in 1841, some years before the police became established in the USA and many years before detection as it is now understood was one of their activities. However, Poe's tale is set in Paris and his detective was C Auguste Dupin, who was the first fictional detective. Paris was a clever choice of venue since the first detective agency was started there in 1811 by the criminalist Eugène François Vidocq with the name *La Sûreté Nationale*. Poe not only knew that there was a detective agency (although the word 'detective' had not yet been coined) but also knew of Vidocq who is referred to by Dupin as a good guesser.

Although Poe may not have chosen to establish the format of a single 'detective' acting alone, that is what he did. Wilkie Collins had as his 'detective' a police sergeant, and wove an intricate plot around a stolen jewel and its subsequent recovery. Once the brilliant Sherlock Holmes and his friend Dr Watson appeared in many short stories and detective novels, the format of the amateur detective acting alone was firmly established; a further touch was the humiliation of the police: it was they who were portrayed as bungling amateurs who could not measure up to the 'ratiocination' skills of the master who had learned his craft from his master at medical school.

Thus when two female authors wrote their first detective stories the format was already established and they followed it. Dorothy Sayers had Lord Peter Wimsey; Agatha Christie had two detectives: a real one, a Belgian called Hercule Poirot and an English busybody called Miss Marple. Each of them worked alone but in a different way. Poirot took ratiocination to a new level; he was not keen on the minutiae of evidence. Not for him being on his knees with a magnifying glass: rather he used psychology and behaviour and his 'little grey cells': a Belgian Dupin. Miss Marple was above all else a gossip and the small items of information that she gleaned from this she skilfully assembled and announced the identity of the criminal.

The interval between the wars was the golden age of crime fiction and eventually the established format morphed slightly; there was still a single brain at work but it was in the skull of a police officer. Two of the great post-war crime novelists were P D James and Ruth Rendall (both of whom died within a few months of each other in 2014/15). James' man, Adam Dalgliesh, rose in rank through her books and ended as a commander; Rendall's man was Chief Inspector Wexford. They were each attached to a police force — Dalgliesh to the Met; Wexford to the fictitious town of Kingsmarkham, but worked largely on their own, Dalgliesh by cerebral means and Wexford by more conventional policing. These detective novels are well written and enjoyable to read but they pay little attention to the reality of how the police work.

This format was continued in the theatre in plays such as *The Mousetrap* and other 'country house' thrillers. The single private detective descends on a house party where a murder has been or is about to be committed, and then either proceeds to solve the mystery single-handedly or is revealed as the culprit.

The fictional single civilian/policeman detective hero did not really change until the advent of film and more particularly television. TV adapted Colin Dexter's books featuring his detective hero Morse, and later featuring Morse's erstwhile side-kick Lewis in two long-running series. But in each, the police stations from which they presumably operated were rarely seen. Writing a crime book featuring the characters in a police station would be a formidable undertaking and the resulting book would be more likely to leave the reader bemused than entertained, let alone enthralled.

Television, however, has no problem with this as series such as *Z Cars*, *The Sweeney* and, in particular, *The Bill*, a three times a week show on ITV, that took place in a fictional police station called Sunhill with a large cast of police officers, demonstrate. Whereas the first two shows just mentioned depicted macho policemen racing around in cars, *The Bill* showed the routine running of a police station that was reasonably true to life. What writers of books could possibly do with difficulty if at all, television can do with ease.

The same is almost as true for courtroom drama. It is perfectly possible for a skilled writer to write a crime novel in which a courtroom scene is central. But unless the writer is very familiar with what goes on inside—and outside—courts it would be quite difficult to hold the reader's attention for long, and it is difficult to imagine a book entirely devoted to a court case. The reason that Harper Lee's courtroom scene in *To Kill A Mockingbird* is so gripping is that the reader knows that the hero of the book is going to lose even though his case is really impregnable.

There are, of course, books written that do contain court scenes. These may be—and be intended to be—funny, like the tales of the barristers' chambers and the Old Bailey featuring Horace Rumpole written by John Mortimer, where the cases portrayed have the structure of real court procedure; or the court tales, short stories and novels written by Henry Cecil, which are usually fairly straight laced, that give an accurate portrayal of court procedure and the occasional wry laugh. But, generally speaking, court scenes between the covers of a book can be very dry.

Some films have successfully incorporated court scenes which are reasonably accurate, but books are not written which are almost entirely taken up with a court trial. Agatha Christie's *Witness for the Prosecution* is an exception, but it is a long short story with a surprise ending which lacks verisimilitude, although it was later made into a stage play and a film.

As discussed above, a number of trial scene plays have been broadcast on TV but they are rarely good enough to sustain interest, and some of them stray beyond what is realistic. The striking exception, to my mind, is *Kavanagh QC* which had the advantage of fine writers and John Thaw in the title role. Unlike trials in books or on stage, television can create a realistic courtroom and make the proceedings authentic even in small details.

Finally there is a topic where the reverse is true: forensic pathology can be presented far better in book form than on television, and has not, so far as I can discern, been attempted on stage. Series such as *Silent Witness*, in which dead bodies somehow reveal their likely murderer using the know-how of young novice pathologists; *Waking the Dead*, whilst having a reasonable police format, becomes unbelievable with their magical 'profiler' and little more than teenage 'forensic pathologists' who are able to conduct any scientific procedures requested.

In contrast, it is difficult to write crime books featuring forensic pathology if the author is not a pathologist. There are two American forensic pathologists who write authentic books, far better than anything seen on television: Patricia Cornwall and Kathy Reichs (who is more of a forensic anthropologist). These two writers are real pathology consultants at the peak of their profession with the ability to write crime fiction in which pathology is central to the plots.

℣

To sum up, writers in any medium do what is possible. In the crime literature, authors picked up on a tradition in which a single person solves the crime; in earlier tales the detective was not a policeman but in later stories he or she often is, although acting alone or with an assistant. Most authors are not equipped to write about large groups of policemen, although a few, such as the American Ed McBain, have done so.

The stage is rarely suitable for plots involving the police, except singly, or court dramas as they are too static. The film and TV media are ideally suited for police dramas, particularly those involving outdoor chases in high-powered cars. Other than books, none of the remaining media have portrayed forensic pathology accurately or even believably; the few books, written by active pathologists, have achieved just that.

In short, where the medium is appropriate to the plot (for example book:

single detective) there is a good chance that the work will be accurate and believable.

Where the medium is not appropriate to the plot (for example television: forensics) the portrayal of the science is false and unbelievable. The medium really is the message.

Bad writing will trump even good plots but not even good writing can overcome a plot written for the wrong medium.

Where the depiction of the police and detectives bears little resemblance to how the police operate in reality; that court procedure is sometimes not a fair portrayal of what goes on in a courtroom; and complex scientific procedures are much over-simplified, it is often because the stories are told in the wrong medium. That is the reason why there is a disjunction between what really goes on and what is written, between fiction and what it purports to represent.

Apart from the disjunction between fiction and reality in terms of accuracy and credibility or actual mistakes there is an even greater difference between fiction and real life.

First, nobody will buy a book, visit a theatre or watch a TV programme about petty shoplifting or driving at an excess speed or being drunk in a public place. Crime fiction in whatever medium is about serious crime, usually involving unnatural death, whereas most real crime is concerned with petty offences. There are about 650 murders a year in the UK but many thousands of driving offences and petty thefts.

Second, there is an even greater disparity between fiction and reality: in fiction, whether literature, the stage or TV and film, the story concludes when the crime is solved; there is invariably a 'happy' ending. (To anyone who is about to point out that Hamlet, King Lear and Antigone had very unhappy endings I would say that they are not primarily crime fiction.) We read a book, watch a play, view television to find out whodunit, which gives us an intellectual satisfaction; the pieces in the end fit together: the author doesn't cheat. But over and above that, subconsciously, subliminally, a solved crime with the criminal safely locked up gives us a sense of closure. The tales we read and watch need a moral base as well as clever detectives. This is rarely available in real life which is one reason for reading and watching crime fiction. The best crime novels depict aspects of the human condition just as well as crime-free fiction does. Who is to say that some of the novels of P D James are not as good as those of Charlotte Brontë or that Patricia Highsmith is not as clever as O Henry?

We seek in crime fiction that which we often lack in real life, and sometimes we find it.

Index

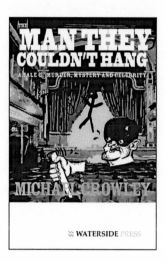
The Man They Couldn't Hang:
A Tale of Murder, Mystery and Celebrity
by Michael Crowley

A play in two Acts with a captivating introduction by the author. The true story of John 'Babbacombe' Lee is one of the most bizarre in English criminal history. Lee is the only person to have cheated the gallows after the trapdoor failed to open. This happened at Exeter Prison in 1885 when the notoriously inept public hangman James Berry gave up after three abortive attempts. Lee spent 22 years in prison before being released. On retirement, Berry took to the boards, spinning gruesome tales of his former trade and showing audiences his dark souvenirs. Michael Crowley's imaginative play is set in a down-at-heel northern music hall where the proprietor is bent on reviving the venue's glory days by persuading the now released John Lee to team up with Berry in a perilous double act.

Paperback & ebook | ISBN 978-1-904380-64-1 | 2010 | 140 pages

Images of Incarceration:
Representations of Prison in Film and Television Drama
by Professor David Wilson and Sean O'Sullivan

Images of Incarceration focuses on fictional portrayals of prison and prisoners to demonstrate how they are depicted in cinema and on TV, featuring films such as *The Shawshank Redemption*, *The Birdman of Alcatraz*, *Scum*, *McVicar*, *Brubaker*, *Cool Hand Luke*, *Made in Britain* and *Greenfingers* as well as TV dramas like *Porridge*, *Bad Girls*, *Buried* and *Oz*. This innovative book compares fictional representations with 'actual existing reality' to provide insights into how screen images affect understanding of complex social and penal issues raising questions such as: 'Is prison really as represented on screen, harsher, softer or different?'; 'Do viewers separate fact from fiction?'; and 'What might films tell us about the experiences of prisoners and whether prison reduces crime and protects victims?'

Paperback & ebook | ISBN 978-1-904380-08-5 | 2004 | 200 pages